BOXING

Training, Skills and Techniques

BOXING

Training, Skills and Techniques

THE CROWOOD PRESS

First published in 2007 by
The Crowood Press Ltd
Ramsbury, Marlborough
Wiltshire SN8 2HR

www.crowood.com

British Library Cataloguing-in-Publication Data
A catalogue record for this book is available from the British Library.

ISBN   978 1 86126 902 7

Unless otherwise credited, all the photographs in this book were taken by
Tony Bates.

Disclaimer

Please note that the author and the publisher of this book are not responsible
in any manner whatsoever for any damage or injury of any kind that may result
from practising, or applying, the principles, ideas, techniques and/or following
the instructions/information described in this publication. Since the physical
activities described in this book, which involve punches to the body and
prolonged physical exercise, may be too strenuous in nature for some readers to
engage in safely, it is essential that a doctor be consulted prior to undertaking
training.

Typeset by S R Nova Pvt Ltd., Bangalore, India

Printed and bound in Spain by GraphyCems

Contents

Foreword

I first really got to know Gary Blower twenty-two years ago, when he came to join our boxing club. The club in question was the Austin Amateur Boxing Club and I was assistant coach to national coach Dennis Jackson. Gary had been boxing for Redditch ABC and whenever he was matched against one of our boxers we always knew they were in for a tough contest. I particularly remember him causing quite an upset when in only his eighth bout, he outboxed and outpointed one of our area champions. A couple of years later he came and joined our team, as he felt he had reached as far as he could with his current club. The Austin was a club steeped in boxing history that had produced many champions at national and multinational level and under Dennis Jackson, Gary became a much better all-round boxer.

He was a very popular and busy boxer who would compete at a minute's notice and never once turned down or pulled out of a contest. Gary would be regularly involved in the best bout of the night on many shows and won endless boxer-of-the-tournament awards. As a model club member, Gary was probably one of the fittest boxers in the gym, who was extremely dedicated and gave one hundred per cent in every bout. He was a very skilful, textbook type of boxer who had a great understanding and knowledge of the sport.

Gary would always be on the wrong end of a close decision and it was due to the character of the man that he would be first in the gym the next day. Although he had a good career in boxing he never quite reached the heights that I felt he was capable of and after over fifty senior bouts he retired from competing.

Due to illness Dennis Jackson retired from coaching and I took over the reins of the club, producing many champions of my own. I renewed my association with Gary ten years later when he asked if I would take a look at a few young prospects he had been coaching at his gym. Week after week he would bring his boxers along to spar and train at my gym and not one of his boxers failed to impress me! The most noticeable thing about each and every one of them was their extreme fitness and dedication and they all gave one hundred per cent, very much in the same mould as Gary. He possesses the same enthusiasm and attitude in schooling and training his boxers as he had when he competed. His boxers are now becoming a major part of my squad, as is Gary, who along with my coaching team and myself hope to continue producing even more champions.

Anyone who reads this book will gain a wonderful insight into the sport of amateur boxing and the preparation required for any boxer to reach competition level. For someone starting out in the sport, the section on training, techniques and nutrition will be most valuable. As an experienced coach of over twenty-five years, I personally found the training section combining old tried and tested methods along with new techniques, most useful.

Micky Redman
ABA Coach

Preface

Saturday 10 October 1981 is a date firmly fixed in the mind of the author. It was on this day at a sold-out Abbey Stadium in Redditch that he boxed competitively for the first time, winning on points and receiving the 'boxer of the night' award. Twenty-five years later Gary is still involved with boxing, training and coaching people of every level. During his boxing career he boxed under the guidance of national coach Dennis Jackson. Dennis was part of the England squad headed by probably one of Britain's most innovative coaches, Kevin Hickey.

It was whilst under the tuition of Dennis that Gary received his grounding towards training competitive boxers. As a fitness instructor for thirty years, Gary has qualified in aerobic fitness, Aerobic and Fitness Association of America (AFAA) weight training, National Amateur Body Building Association (NABBA) and Olympic Lifting, British Amateur Weight Lifting Association (BAWLA). At the age of twenty he managed his first health club, that at this time was the largest of its kind in the United Kingdom. In 1997 he opened his own fitness centre specializing in boxing training and conditioning, where people could learn the art of boxing away from the competitive atmosphere of an amateur boxing club. Working with small groups of boxers or on a one-to-one basis, with his knowledge of training and experience in competing, Gary can teach and prepare any youngsters who may have ambitions and the ability to compete. Many of the boxers he has trained have now filtered through to competitive level, with more and more almost up to that standard.

The author, Gary Blower.

Introduction

Boxing training is widely regarded as one of the hardest forms of training there is. It is due to this fact that many people of all ages and levels of fitness are using the training methods of a boxer as a way of improving their physical condition.

This book will be a useful guide to anyone wishing to participate in a boxing-based programme, purely to learn new skills and improve their overall fitness. The core of this book is dedicated to the amateur side of boxing and in particular the amateur boxer. Anyone with aspirations of boxing competitively will almost certainly go through their local amateur boxing club. There is, of course, a major difference between training for wellbeing and training to compete, as the competitive boxer has to be totally dedicated and, at the same time, extremely fit and focused.

For any up-and-coming boxers reading this book, they will find it useful in helping to understand what is required to box competitively. The technical and training advice given throughout the book has all been tried and tested on boxers of all levels, but they are only guidelines and competitive boxers will need to consult their coaches before attempting any new methods. To a boxing purist the amateur code is often regarded as the true sport of boxing, where a contest between two amateur boxers is not a fight but a challenge of skill.

Amateur boxing is one of the last sports in England that can be truly called amateur, but for a boxer to reach the top at international level, he must train and discipline himself as hard or even harder than any other professional athlete. After thirty years' involvement in the sport, firstly as a competitive amateur boxer and then as a trainer, the author knows how much a boxer sacrifices just to compete at any level.

He has long been a fan of Cuban and Russian amateur boxing and is a great admirer of their disciplined coaching methods, which enables them to nurture young and raw talent into World and Olympic Champions. His first memory of amateur boxing was watching Chris Finnegan win a gold medal for Great Britain in the 1968 Olympics in Mexico. Since then Audley Harrison is the only other British boxer to have won an Olympic gold, that being in Sydney, Australia 2000.

The author truly hopes and believes that with the right funding and the standard of coaching and young talent that is now filtering through, England will soon be amongst the top boxing nations.

CHAPTER 1

The Sport of Boxing

IN THE BEGINNING

Man has fought man since the beginning of time, and the first indication of any form of boxing dates back as far as 4000BC. Egyptian heiroglyphics show soldiers fighting with hands and forearms bound, and ancient Greek vases and murals display fighters with wrist and fingers bandaged. These were the early forms of the boxing glove. To describe this type of combat the word 'Pugilisim' was introduced, from the Greek 'pugme' through the Latin 'Pugilatas', the art of fighting with fists and also 'pugnus', a fight.

Fighters participating were known as Pugilists and the term 'Boxing' came from the clenching of the fist with the fingers turned into the palm of the hand and the thumb positioned in line with the fingers to lay along the fingers to form a box. In ancient Greece the god Apollon was considered the patron saint of boxing. Apollon the body beautiful, was the son of Zeus and Leto and defeated Ares, the god of war, in a contest where Zeus acted as match-maker, therefore known as *puktus* (boxer).

In 2500BC the Greeks created a sport known as 'pankration', which was a combination of wrestling and boxing. This was included in the twenty-third ancient Olympics for the first time in 668BC, when Onomatos of Smyria became the very first Olympic boxing champion. The first officially recorded Olympics were held in 776BC in honour of Zeus.

Later the sport was introduced to the Romans, who used a brutal form of boxing glove known as a caestus. The caestus had originally been used by the Greeks, but now the Romans had added iron or brass studs, causing the death of many a fighter.

It is believed that it was the Romans who introduced the first form of fist fighting to Britain, and

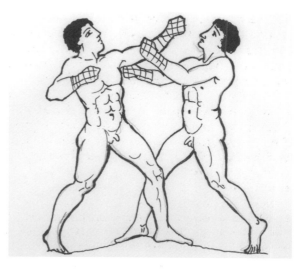

Pankration, a combination of wrestling and boxing.

by the seventeenth century bare-knuckle prize fighting had started to become popular in these islands. Fights would take place mostly at travelling fairs and on village greens with the crowd forming a circle holding a rope. This was how the boxing ring originated. Bouts were often brutal and some contests lasted for hours with over one hundred rounds sometimes being fought. A round would end when one of the fighters went down, and the contest would continue until one fighter was knocked out or in no position to continue due to injuries or pure exhaustion.

It was in the early part of the eighteenth century when boxing in Britain really became popular, mainly due to the exploits of the British heavyweight champion of 1719, James Figg. Figg opened a boxing academy where he advertised the teaching

Bare-knuckle boxer Bill Richmond, known as the 'Black Terror', demonstrates the typical stance of the prize fighter in the eighteenth century.

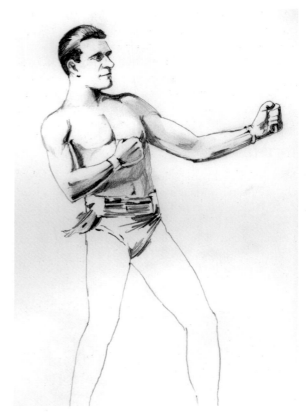

Gentleman Jim Corbett, the first heavyweight champion of the world.

of boxing and sparring exhibitions. A master swordsman, Figg also taught gentlemen in the use of the small backsword and the quarter staff. After the opening of Figg's school many more academies started to appear, using wooden rails in place of ropes to form a ring. The ring would be elevated upon a stage and the referee would officiate from outside the ring.

The title was won by Jack Broughton in 1734 when, during his reign as champion, he fought George Stevenson in a brutal fight. So severe was the beating that Broughton enflicted on Stevenson that he died from his injuries. It was due to the tragic events of this fight that Broughton drew up the first set of rules to govern boxing. Broughton, who had his own boxing academy, also invented the padded boxing gloves that were known as mufflers, but these were only used in sparring exhibitions. Broughton's rules stood from 1743 until 1838 when 'The London Queensberry Prize Ring Rules' came

into force. In 1866 The Marquis of Queensberry Rules were introduced and contests were now boxed over three-minute rounds and 5oz gloves would be worn. The first heavyweight champion of the world under Queensberry Rules was Gentleman Jim Corbett who beat fellow American John L. Sullivan, the last great bareknuckle champion, in the twenty-first round by knock-out in 1892. James J. Corbett not only became the first heavyweight champion of the world, but he brought science into a sport that was usually associated with a slugging, brawling style of fighting. Corbett was a technical fighter and used such tactics as slick defensive movement and skilful footwork. Standing at 6ft 1in and weighing 178lb, Corbett could out-think and frustrate most of his opponents, as well as possessing a powerful punch.

Educated and always smartly dressed, the dapper self-confident Corbett was known as Gentleman Jim Corbett throughout his career.

Seventy-two years later another brash young boxer became a heavyweight champion of the world – his name was Cassius Clay. Clay like Corbett changed the face of heavyweight boxing with his fancy footwork and the blistering speed of his hands. Born in Louisville, Kentucky in 1942, Clay soon earned the nickname of the 'Louisville Lip' because of his fast talking and boastful chants of 'I am the greatest'. Like Corbett when he fought Sullivan, Clay also had to face a powerful hard-hitting champion in Sonny Liston to become heavyweight king. The bout took place on 25 February 1964 in Miami and against all odds the 21-year-old Clay became heavyweight champion of the world when Liston failed to come out for the seventh round. After becoming the champion, Clay converted to Islam and changed his name to Muhammad Ali. Ali had a long, successful career and became the first man to win the heavyweight championship of the world on three occasions. Today Muhammad Ali is not only recognized as the best boxer of all time, but also 'The Greatest' sportsmen ever.

As well as bringing style and finesse into the world of boxing, Ali and Corbett both added showmanship and entertainment to the sport. They were both introduced into boxing through the amateurs with Corbett having a successful amateur career until he turned professional at the age of nineteen. Ali had his first amateur bout when he was twelve and went on to win a gold medal at light heavyweight in the 1960 Olympics in Rome. Most top professional champions today have had success in the amateur ranks and that is why amateur boxing plays such an important role in the sport and is the backbone of boxing.

THE AMATEUR CODE

From 1867 an amateur championship had taken place with just three weights being contested, lightweight, middle- and heavyweight. The competitions were fought under the Marquis of Queensberry Rules and in 1880 the Amateur Boxing Association was formed, drawing up sixteen rules. These rules covered the judging system and awarded points to the boxer scoring the most attacking hits, with the knuckle part of the glove on their opponent's head or body above the belt.

In 1906 all amateur boxers had to have a medical examination before competing. This is a practice that has continued right up to the modern day. All amateur boxers must have a medical book before they are allowed to compete. This book, which is called an ME3, will have a record of all the boxer's matches up-to-date and will be shown to the officiating doctor before each contest. All boxers will have a medical examination prior to every contest and will have had a full medical by their local doctor before they are issued with their medical book.

Due to the pure nature of the sport, boxing can be dangerous, but amateur boxing is way down the list of high-risk sports. During a contest the referee is the sole person in charge. The referee's main concern is for the safety of the boxers and he will stop a contest if he feels it is too one-sided, or if one of the boxers is injured. Referees can also administer a standing eight count should they feel a boxer is hurt but has remained standing. At any time during a contest the referee can consult with the ringside doctor for advice on a boxer's wellbeing. Contests range from three to four rounds depending on the age and class categories. International and championship bouts between

Classified Boxing Weights – Senior Level

Light-Fly 48kg (106lb)
Fly 51kg (112lb)
Bantam 54kg (119lb)
Feather 57kg (126lb)
Light 60kg (132lb)
Light-Welter 64kg (141lb)
Welter 69kg (152lb)
Middle 75kg (165lb)
Light-Heavy 81kg (179lb)
Heavy 91kg (201lb)
Super-Heavy 91$^+$kg (201$^+$lb)

All weights are the maximum for each category, with the exception of super heavyweight, which has no limit.

Amateur boxers in the twenty-first century.

1992 Amateur Boxing Association of England, ABAE champion Mark Santini, receiving a winner's trophy at a club show.

open class boxers will be held over four two-minute rounds. Intermediate and novice boxers will mostly compete over three two-minute rounds. School children between the age of eleven and thirteen will box three one-and-a-half-minute rounds. At every level there is a one-minute interval between rounds.

The ABA Championships are the domestic highlight for all top amateur boxers in Britain. For the ambitious boxer, winning an ABA title can be a great springboard for bigger and better things. Professional world champions such as Randolph Turpin, Ken Buchanan, John Conteh, Charlie Magri, Alan Minter, Frank Bruno, Ricky Hatton and Joe Calzaghe to name but a few were all former ABA champions. The first ABA championship ever staged was in 1881 with only four weights being contested, featherweight, lightweight, middleweight and heavyweight. The competition has moved a long way since then and England, Scotland, Ireland and Wales all hold their own ABA championships. Each champion from each weight and nation meet in the Four Nations Tournament. The winner of each weight category can then truly be called British and Irish champion.

Boxing for Your Country

Every amateur boxer dreams of boxing for his country and having the opportunity to represent your country is a great honour. The four major international tournaments for British amateur boxers are the European Championships, the World Championships, the Commonwealth Games and the Olympic Games.

The Olympics are the pinnacle of every amateur boxer's career, but for a British boxer to be selected he must qualify through either the European or World Championships. This is not an easy task when you consider he will be up against boxers from Cuba and Russia whose countries give amateur boxing a high priority and where boxing is state supported. Britain's tally of gold medals has been pretty scarce, with just four winners since 1948: Terry Spinks and Dick McTaggart in Melbourne 1956, Chris Finnegan in Mexico City 1968 and Audley Harrison in Sydney 2000.

England international Jimmy Moran, winner of the light-heavyweight Commonwealth Games gold medal in Edinburgh 1986.

Jimmy Moran receives instructions from national coach Ian Irwin in between rounds, during an international tournament.

Britain's only representative in the 2004 Games in Athens was seventeen-year-old Amir Khan. Khan had qualified as junior World Champion and was only having his fourteenth senior bout when he boxed in the Olympic final. Khan's opponent was one of the all-time greats in amateur boxing, 33-year-old Cuban Mario Kindélan. Kindélan was the defending Olympic Champion and three times World Champion. His silky skills and masterful boxing were too much for the game Khan, who lost thirty points to twenty-two points giving him a well-deserved silver medal.

The Cubans

In Athens, as in many Olympics, the Cuban boxers came out on top with five gold medals with Russia close behind with three. As previously mentioned, these countries take amateur boxing very seriously. Cuba has dominated international amateur boxing for three decades, winning thirty Olympic gold medals since Munich 1972. This is an amazing achievement considering Cuba boycotted the 1984 and 1988 Olympics. Four years previous to their five gold medals at Athens they had been top, winning four gold medals in Melbourne. So the Cubans do not seem to be losing their dominance, but why are they so good?

You have to go back to 1962 when Cuba's communist leader, Fidel Castro, banned all professional sports. This meant that none of the top amateur stars were lost to professional boxing. Boxing in Cuba is state-funded and their top boxers are treated to houses and cars that a lot of their fellow citizens can only dream of. Castro is a big boxing fan and when Mario Kindélan won his gold medal in Athens, he was rewarded with a brand new car. The man behind the Cuban boxing success was coach Alcides Sagarra, who took charge in 1964. Also the Soviet coach, Andrei Chervorenko, played a large part in the development of Cuban boxing teams by enforcing strict Soviet training methods. Sagarra and Chervorenko managed to blend the natural rhythm and ability of the Cubans with Soviet discipline to produce world-beating boxing teams year after year. Sagarra finally stepped down as coach in 2001 leaving behind a legacy of amateur boxing's finest.

The biggest name in Cuban boxing has to be Teofilo Stevenson; in Cuba the man is simply a legend. Stevenson won three Olympic gold medals and two World Championships at heavyweight before moving up to superheavyweight in 1986 to win yet another World Championship. During the 1970s professional promoters tried to put together a match between Stevenson and Muhammad Ali, billing it as the world's greatest amateur heavyweight against the world's greatest professional heavyweight. The fight never took place and Stevenson's mantle was finally taken over by 6ft 6in-heavyweight Felix Savon. Savon also won three Olympic golds and was World Champion an amazing five times. He resisted promoter Don King's offer of ten million dollars to turn professional. Savon's answer to King's proposal was, 'What do I need ten million dollars for when I have eleven million Cubans behind me...'. It is this passion for their country and for boxing that makes Cuba such a dominant force. Some boxers do try and defect but most believe in the battle cry 'Don't fight for money, fight for Cuba, Don't fight for fame, fight for pride, Viva Cuba, viva Fidel!'

A lot of international coaches argue that if they did not lose their top boxers to the professional ranks, they, too, would produce much stronger national teams. There is a lot of truth in this but Cuba's success does not just come from the banning of professional sports. Cuba, like Russia, nurtures its talented boxers from an early age, placing them into state-sponsored athletic schools and training camps. The programme outlined for these youngsters is tough and disciplined but failure is not an option and winning is everything.

The Boxer

Britain's youngsters begin boxing seriously at around the ages of eleven and twelve when they can enter the school championships. Of course, people take to the sport at various ages but amateur boxing rules prohibit boxers competing after the age of thirty-four. So if you are hoping for a long career in the amateurs, the earlier you start the better.

Two schoolboys sparring. Boxers can start competing from the age of eleven.

People walk into their local boxing clubs for many reasons. Some want to get fit, some want to use boxing as a way of channeling their aggression, others just want to keep off the streets. Some have dreams of winning an Olympic gold or becoming a professional World Champion one day, but whatever the reason, the first time you walk into a boxing gym can be quite a daunting experience. ABA clubs are usually full to the rafters with young boxers going through their training routines. Amongst this crowd of sweating, panting bodies are two or three enthusiastic coaches attempting to be everywhere at once. As you enter the gym for the first time one of these coaches will make themselves known by demonstrating a few pointers to help get you started. In reality, amateur coaches give their time for free and after putting in a full day at work they will always be found down at the gym most nights of the week. When not at the club they are usually with their boxers at one of the many shows in the UK. Once the coach sees that the boxer has the same level of commitment to the sport that they themselves have, they will then give much more of their time. The boxer will then be put through one of the hardest training regimes of any sport.

For a boxer to reach a competitive level he has to be superbly fit, both physically and mentally and must be completely dedicated. Along with increased fitness and strength comes an understanding of boxing technique. Once the boxer has grasped the basic fundamentals of the sport and shows some ability, he will then be tested against other boxers of the same age group, weight and experience through the practice of sparring. Most coaches can evaluate a great deal from these early sessions, monitoring the reaction of each boxer once they get hit for the first time. For the young boxer, sparring is the first real taste of what boxing is all about.

Boxing can be a hurtful sport and not only in the physical sense. Obviously, any sport where you score points for punching your opponent involves enduring some pain. Most boxers can deal with the black eyes, split lips and aching head but the real hurt is being on the end of a losing decision when you believe you have won hands down. There is also the disappointment of training for weeks for a contest, keeping to a strict diet so you can make the weight and then going all the way to the venue after having butterflies in your stomach all day, only to be told your opponent has pulled out of the bout for one reason or another. This is why boxing is known to be character building, as a person needs strong willpower to put these disappointments behind them and be back in the gym the next day.

The sport of boxing is hard and is known as the hardest game, but boxing is far from a game. Once you are in that ring and the bell goes you are on your own. Against your opponent there are no team-mates behind you to rely on.

Boxing does have its critics who believe that the sport does not have a place in modern society. Everybody knows boxing can be dangerous, but if people cannot understand the sport, they will never be able to accept the benefits that it offers. Benefits such as taking youngsters off the street and giving them some self-belief and confidence. Because of its character-building attributes and because it teaches controlled aggression, it has always ranked high on the criteria in the combined services. In the Army, boxers represent their regiment against other regiments, with the top boxers gaining selection to box for the British Army. This also applies to the Royal Navy and to the Royal Air Force. Those servicemen who participate in boxing regard it as a great honour.

Army boxer Jake Spencer of the Royal Fusiliers, prepares for the novice championships at Gary's gym.

The British amateur rankings are always well represented by all three services, with many going on to win national honours and even international selection.

There are hundreds of ABA clubs around Britain with thousands of registered boxers. Only a handful of these will make it to the top level, winning national championships and even fewer will gain medals representing their country. The real spine of the ABA is the hundreds of novice boxers who regularly compete in the many club shows that are staged. These boxers may compete for many years and still box in the novice category, but without them amateur boxing would not survive. Novice boxers may never experience the glory of the open class boxers, but a national novice championship takes place annually giving new boxers a chance to compete for a title, hopefully leading on to bigger challenges.

Gary in the white vest competing during the mid-1980s, before the introduction of compulsory wearing of headguards.

More women are now participating in the once male-only sport of boxing.

In the last twenty years amateur boxing has undergone many changes, such as the introduction of headguards to be worn in all contests and computerized electronic scoring systems for all major tournaments. Although these new additions to the sport were in their way not that radical, some of the tradionalists took time to accept them. But like all sports, boxing has had to move on and these new rulings have not taken away any of the excitement.

The change that really shook the foundations of the amateur code was the inclusion of female boxers. Women had been accepted in nearly all male-dominated sports, such as cricket, football and rugby for many years, but boxing has always kept its doors firmly closed on the ladies. Girls were not strangers to combat sport as they had always participated in martial arts such as judo and karate, but in boxing it was only males who were allowed to compete under ABA rules.

Professional women's boxing started to hit the headlines in the 1990s with boxers like America's Christy Martin who fought Ireland's Deidre Gogarty on a Mike Tyson fight bill in 1996. The contest was watched by an estimated 1.1 million viewers, instantly making women's boxing more popular.

In Britain Jane Couch pioneered women's boxing by becoming World Champion and going on to be the first female boxer to hold a British Boxing Board of Control (BBBC) licence. In 2001 the great Muhammad Ali's daughter Laila competed with her father's great rival's, Joe Frazier's daughter, Jacqueline. Ali won an eight-round decision in front of 6,500 fans. In 1993 America permitted female boxers to compete against other female boxers in amateur sanctioned competitions. The Amateur International Boxing Association (AIBA) included female boxing in its programme in 1994. The first female bout in Britain took place in 1997. By the year 2000 thirty-four countries practised female boxing. The USA held the first-ever women's World Championships in 2001 and there were big hopes that female boxing would be sanctioned in the 2004 Olympics. Unfortunately, the women boxers were left disappointed as they were not included in the Athens games. Beijing 2008 is the target for all the top female amateurs, as they push to achieve Olympic recognition. Female boxing will never have the number of participants, nor the following of male boxing, but people who are involved in the sport have had to admit that female boxers are not a novelty, but are indeed dedicated and talented athletes who deserve the same respect as their male counterparts.

Amateur v Professional

Nearly every professional boxer has learnt his trade competing for his local amateur club. Although professionals usually start in the ABA clubs, once they have decided to box for money, instead of trophies and cups, they begin to experience the difference between the two codes. Besides boxing minus headguards and vests, they will also find the pace of professional boxing totally different. The speed of amateur boxing is much faster as there are less rounds than in the pro-game, leaving the amateur less time to settle into a contest. Novice professionals will usually compete over four, or six, two-minute rounds but as the boxer gains more experience the duration of a round will go up to three minutes. Seasoned professionals will compete over eight to ten rounds with championship bouts contested over twelve rounds.

Besides the brisker pace of the amateur, the style of the amateur boxer is often seen as very different from that of the professional. When analysing a boxer's ability many observers may describe a particular boxer as having a typical amateur style. This is not meant as an insult but implies the boxer in question boxes with a very upright stance, moving in and out of his opponent, working behind their jab. Of course, it is not always the case as boxers have various styles, but many coaches try to encourage their boxers to adopt this technique.

In amateur boxing the emphasis is on point scoring with points being gained once a boxer has landed a correct punch on his opponent. As already mentioned, judges now use the electronic scoring system, where five judges feed the computer by pressing their respective buttons for scoring punches. For a punch to score, at least three of the five judges will need to have pressed their button within one second of each other. The boxer landing the single cleaner punches is often more likely to catch the judge's eye. Amateurs when knocking down an opponent will gain just one point where professionals will get the full maximum ten points for that round. In addition to the new computer system a hand-held scoring machine has also been introduced. Each machine has a red and blue button that represents each boxer. When a boxer scores with a blow the judge presses the appropriate button. Once the bout has finished, each judge records his score on the score paper and hands it to a referee.

Unlike in the amateurs there is no standing eight count in professional boxing in Britain. With both the professionals and amateurs a knock-out is awarded when a boxer has put his opponent down on the floor for the referee's count of ten. Many of Britain's top amateurs turn professional due to a lack of sponsorship and recognition. Some adopt very well even going all the way to world titles, but some fall at their first serious hurdle. Also you sometimes find that boxers who had limited success as an amateur are really well suited to the professional style of boxing. It is interesting to note that of the twenty-one British boxers who have won medals in the Olympics since the War, only three have won world titles as professionals. The three were Alan Minter, Robin Reid and Richie Woodall and all three were bronze medallists.

In 2004, mainly due to Amir Khan's success in the Olympics of that year, the ABA came to the conclusion that to prevent their top boxers converting to the professional ranks, amateur boxers needed to be financially subsidized. Also in that same year barriers between the ABA and BBBC began to come down, as both parties agreed on pro-am shows.

Amateur boxers have been appearing on professional boxing bills in countries such as Germany, Italy and France for many years, giving young boxers a chance to experience a big show atmosphere. This move by the ABA to link with

Gary with ex-professional and amateur star Pat Cowdell. Pat won two ABA titles, a Commonwealth gold medal, a European bronze medal and an Olympic bronze medal. As a professional he won British and European titles.

British Professional Weight Divisions

Weight	Stone/lb	kg
Flyweight	8st 0lb	50.8kg
Bantamweight	8st 6lb	53.4kg
Super Bantamweight	8st 10lb	55.5kg
Featherweight	9st 0lb	57.2kg
Super Featherweight	9st 4lb	59.0kg
Lightweight	9st 9lb	61.2kg
Light Welterweight	10st 0lb	63.5kg
Welterweight	10st 7lb	66.7kg
Light Middleweight	11st 0lb	69.9kg
Middleweight	11st 6lb	72.6kg
Super Middleweight	12st 0lb	76.2kg
Light Heavyweight	12st 7lb	79.4kg
Cruiser Weight	14st 4lb	90.7kg
Heavyweight	Over 14st 4lb	90.7kg

professional promoters was seen as a huge step forward towards giving British amateur boxing and its boxers the national exposure they need.

Unfortunately, pro-am shows have yet to transpire and amateur boxing lost its biggest star Amir Khan to the professional ranks. Khan announced his decision live on television immediately after defeating his Olympic conqueror Mario Kindélan in front of his own fans in Bolton on 14 May 2005.

At one time amateur boxers were not permitted to have had any involvement in a professional sport whatsoever. New rulings by the ABA allow the amateur to dip his toe into the water of the professional ranks. An amateur boxer can now compete in a handful of paid bouts, but if after four contests he decides it is not for him, he can return to the amateur code.

The Recreational Boxer

We have already established earlier in this chapter that boxing is a complex sport, where skill is matched against strength. Competitive boxers must have both these attributes, but above all they must be extremely fit, not only physically but mentally. It is because of these requirements that people have turned to boxing for their regular exercise routine.

Boxing gyms are seen as an exclusive club whose doors are only open to a strange breed of fighting men. A general perception is that amateur clubs have little time for people wanting to use the gym as a way of keeping fit, with no intention of ever boxing for their club. Most professional gyms are regarded as 'no go' areas for the novice, as men training to earn their money in the hardest sport of all do not take kindly to a stranger hogging the heavy bag. However, although this may have been the case a few years ago it is certainly not true today.

New York in the 1980s witnessed a trend in which the stockbrokers and bankers of the city were heading towards their nearest boxing gym. By working to a structured boxing training programme in their lunch hour or after work, they found that it helped to unload the stress and tension of their working day. Trainers at these gyms soon saw that there was a market for teaching these Wall Street financial 'whizz kids' how to box for real. Some of these city high flyers were coached and trained to a high standard enabling them to compete against each other, and competitions in front of a paying public were organized under special rules and guidelines. It didn't matter that most of these matches resembled very little that could be called boxing; these highly stressed money men were discovering a way to burn off their excess energy and frustrations and so 'White Collar Boxing' was born. Some organizers in Britain latched onto the idea, staging shows around the country with a lot of the profits going to various charities.

The ABA of England at first were not in favour of this type of contest, but in an effort to attract a wider audience to amateur boxing some White Collar bouts have now taken place on amateur club shows. Most people who participate in boxing training for recreational reasons will never compete or even take part in any sparring sessions, but they are learning a new skill, are getting very fit and channeling their aggression. There has been a big rise in ladies wanting to take up this once male-dominated sport and a lot of women now see boxing as an opportunity to keep fit, lose weight and relieve stress.

COMPETITION ATTIRE

Most boxing clubs supply their boxers with the correct equipment to get them started in their

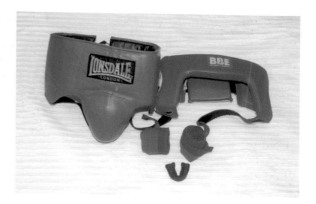

Competition protective clothing and equipment.

quest to compete. All clubs will have a range of bag and sparring gloves, headguards and foul protectors. If you reach competitive standards and you can afford to, it is an advantage to buy your own equipment. Besides the obvious hygiene factors, it is necessary that a boxer's attire is well fitting and causes him no distractions.

Shorts and Vest
Amateur boxing clubs will have their own club colours and will provide the boxer with shorts and vest. Some boxers like to have their own shorts, which may have their name embroidered on them. Shorts are usually velvet or silk and must reach at least half way down the boxer's thigh with the vest covering the chest and back.

Boxing Boots
There are many makes of boxing boots on the market with various styles, but the preferred choice is entirely up to the boxer. It is, however, very important that the boots fit well and are comfortable, light and support the ankle.

Headguard
The boxer's head protection needs to be well fitted and it is vital that it is neither too tight, causing discomfort, nor loose enough for it to slip down the head restricting the boxer's vision. In a contest, if the head protector becomes displaced too often the referee can stop the bout in favour of the

opponent. Competition headguards must be ABAE approved.

Cup Protector

A boxer must always wear a foul protector, which is worn under the shorts. Its purpose is to protect the boxer from punches that have strayed low. This is known as 'below the belt', the belt being the imaginary line from the navel to the top of the hips. Hitting your opponent in that area is seen as a foul blow.

Gumshield

The purpose of the gumshield is to protect the mouth and teeth and it must be worn in all competitions. Gumshields can be tailor-made by a dentist or purchased from most sport retailers. It is essential that the mouth piece fits tightly into the boxer's mouth, as in a contest a boxer faces disqualification if the mouth piece keeps dislodging. Gumshields now come in various colours but red gumshields are forbidden.

Hand Wraps

The boxer needs to protect his hands as they are the most important tool of his trade. Before even punching a bag in training a boxer must wrap his hands, as any knuckle damage can plague him throughout his career.

In competition the rules state 'a crepe-type bandage or approved boxing wrap not longer than 2.5m (8ft 3in) nor wider than 5cm (2in) may be used'. The use of any kind of tapes, or rubber or adhesive plaster as a bandage is strictly forbidden. A single strip of adhesive not to exceed 7.6cm (3in) in length and 2.5cm (1in) in width may be used at the upper wrist to secure the bandage or wrap.

The method each coach favours in wrapping his boxer's hands can vary, but it is vital that his wrist and knuckles are well protected.

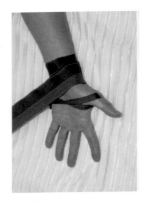

The wrapping of the hands. Coaches will have various methods of wrapping their boxers' hands but the wrist and knuckles must be protected.

Bandages should not be wrapped too tightly around the boxer's hands as to cause him too much discomfort, but they also must not be too loose. Although adhesive tape is not permitted to be used around the hands in competition, due to the constant pounding they endure in the gym, it is advisable to help protect the hands with tape during training.

CHAPTER 2
Basic Techniques

The style that a boxer adopts is determined by a number of factors. Their build, height, personality and temperament are instrumental in the development of their physical and psychological skills. For example a tall, slim, rangy boxer is unlikely to choose a crouching, brawling approach in his boxing. It would be just as unusual for a smaller more muscularly built boxer to box at long range behind a rapier-type jab. A good coach will be able to assess the most effective way for his charge to box, but many boxers will adopt the style most natural to them. For instance, the shorter boxer will often take on the role of the fighter when matched against a taller opponent. He will have the tendency to stand squarer to his opponent with his body weight towards the front foot whilst working behind a two-fisted attack. A taller boxer will use his height advantage against a smaller opponent, working at long range behind his jab with the body weight on the back foot.

For a boxer to develop his perfect stance, he must work from the feet upwards. Positioning of the feet is vitally important, as they will move the boxer in and out of striking distance. Once an individual's style has been acknowledged by the coach, it will be his role to adopt a stance and guard most suited to his boxer. A coach's major concerns are that their boxer's stance and guard provide him with protection at all times. The golden rule in boxing is to hit your opponent whilst not being hit yourself. This sounds logical, but every time a boxer throws a punch he opens up his own defence, leaving parts of the body exposed. Once the boxer has thrown a punch against an opponent he must be fully guarded against the counter-punch. Counter-punching is when the boxer has defended against an attack and immediately launches a strike of his own. So, it is of the utmost importance that once a punch has been thrown the attacking boxer brings his hand back into the guarded position as quickly as possible.

Two boxers of the same weight category, but possessing entirely different builds and styles.

Orthodox Stance and Guard

When the boxer leads with his left hand it is known as orthodox. The orthodox stance is the most commonly used by boxers as opposed to the southpaw, which leads with the right. It is usually accepted that the southpaw is left-handed, but it is not always the case. Some right-handed boxers may adopt this style to give them an advantage over an orthodox boxer. For maximum protection the boxer should have a sideways stance with hands held high in a relaxed style. Elbows are tucked into the side of the body with the head tilted slightly downwards whilst looking up through the eyebrows. The chin will gain cover from the left shoulder. Good vision between the guard is needed at all times, allowing a clear view of the opponent. The body is balanced between the front and back legs and the boxer will need to possess the ability and mobility to enable him to shift his body weight from side to side and front to back for evasion and attack. Feet should be approximately shoulder-width apart allowing a solid base for movement and stability. His front foot should be about 45 degrees from his opponent with the sole of his feet remaining on the floor and his front knee slightly flexed. The back foot is turned slightly more outwards with the heel raised at all times and knee flexed.

The orthodox stance.

The side view.

The Southpaw

We have already covered the difference between the southpaw and an orthodox boxer but every technique in this book can be adapted to the southpaw. All the same principles apply but the opposite way round, like a mirror image. Many southpaws are counter-punches but, like the orthodox boxer, they come in all different types and styles. To the orthodox boxer a southpaw often presents an awkward opponent and plenty of time and work is needed in the gym to prepare oneself to compete against a southpaw. Because there are far more orthodox boxers in comparison to the southpaw a left-handed boxer will always have the bonus of sparring with a larger selection of orthodox boxers,

The southpaw boxer is often an awkward opponent for the orthodox boxer.

giving him an advantage when meeting in contests. Having said this, more and more southpaw boxers appear to be entering the sport. In the 2005 World Championships in China a southpaw featured in almost every bout from the semi-finals through to the finals. It would seem unlikely that all these boxers would be naturally left-handed, so it could be that many right-handed boxers are being encouraged to adopt a right-hand lead stance. For the amateur sport this can be a major bonus in the point-scoring system, as they are leading with their naturally stronger arm.

Basic Footwork and Balance

Footwork in boxing is a variety of short sliding movements allowing a boxer to transfer his body weight forwards or sideways, whilst also enabling him to quickly change and move in various directions. The art of good footwork is having the ability to move forwards, backwards, left and right at speed whilst maintaining good balance. Balance is an integral part of boxing, as poor balance would leave a boxer at a major disadvantage when rolling and slipping punches, making him an easy target for his opponent.

If off balance, punching power will decrease as well as leaving the boxer vulnerable against counter-punches. Learning footwork and co-ordination is like learning to dance, as rhythm

The southpaw stance.

plays an influential part in all movements. When moving forwards the front foot will lead, acting as the range finder, whilst pushing off the back foot, which is the boxer's power driver. With backward movements push off the front foot, while leading with the back foot. The left foot slides first when moving to the left, quickly followed by the right to ensure good balance and a well-guarded stance. Moving to the right the same step will apply, but leading with the right foot with the left foot following. When punching, the punch follows the foot and good form must be enforced at all times. Stance should never be too wide or too narrow, nor should the front and rear foot be directly in line with one another or the legs cross over each other. Having the feet out of position would affect natural movement and balance, whilst reducing punching power.

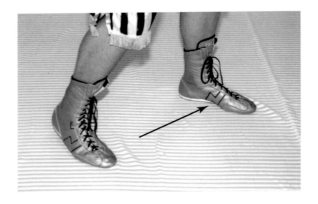

Moving forward, lead with the front foot (the range finder)...

...whilst pushing off with the back foot (the power driver).

The feet should provide a solid base, with the heel of the back foot always raised. Stance should never be too wide or too narrow.

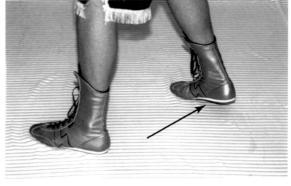

Moving backwards, lead with the back foot...

...followed by the front foot.

Moving to the left, lead with the left foot...

...quickly followed by the right foot to maintain the boxer's stance. When moving to the right lead with the right foot, followed by the left foot.

Punching Technique

Points are scored in amateur boxing by landing punches with the knuckle part of the glove on an opponent's target area. The target area is the front of the head and the body above the belt. Punches landing on shoulders and arms do not score. A landing blow must be delivered with sufficient force for the punch to count. To make a fist the thumb tucks around the fingers between the knuckles and fingernails, keeping the fist tightly clenched when making contact. When launching the punch there is a drive off the back foot whilst twisting the trunk of the body, rotating on the central axis of the body. With a straight

When making a fist, ensure thumb is tucked around the fingers.

The boxing glove – to score with a punch the white part of the glove must make contact with the target.

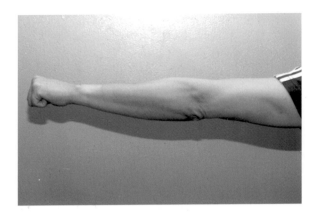

Straight punches are the first punch taught to a boxer. The punch is driven from the shoulder, accelerating towards the target area. Fist and arm are relaxed until contact.

The target area. Any punches landing with sufficient force above the waistband, excluding arms and shoulders are point scorers.

punch the wrist twists before impact with the palm of the hand facing downwards. A perfect punch consists of leg extension, hip rotation and arm extension. The passive hand must stay in defence mode until the striking hand has made contact and returned to its source, keeping the elbow forward. The development of speed and power should place emphasis on foot speed and leg power as faster feet make faster hands.

It needs to be taught early in a boxer's education that every punch thrown does not have to be a knock-out blow. Boxers who use too much force behind every punch will soon run out of energy. Force will be required with every scoring punch, but how much the boxer applies will be dependent on his opponent. Far more energy will be exhausted with punches that have missed the target than ones that have landed. To connect correctly with a striking blow, a punch will need speed and acceleration as it approaches the target. Sufficient force behind the blow must be applied and the punch must be accurate and well-timed. Boxers need the ability to judge distance from the scoring hand and target, keeping the attacking arm relaxed until the last few inches before contact, when the punch will then accelerate to its target.

Breathing

For the punch to have explosive power, it is important that correct breathing technique is taught by the coach as soon as the first punch is thrown in the gym. The heavy grunting-type breathing that is often heard during a contest is not used for effect, but serves an important purpose. By exhaling either through the nose or mouth when delivering punches, or even both will add power to the punch. For example, when tennis players serve the ball or field athletes throw the shot-put or javelin, their explosive breathing will assist with their explosive power. Not only will correct breathing improve the effort of attacking punches, but it will increase the ability to absorb punches, especially in the abdomen area. It is important to remember that breathing has to be controlled and should not be too loud or exaggerated as this could be seen by the referee as a ploy to intimidate or confuse an opponent.

This section will explain the various punches and how to correctly administer them, but also just as important, how to defend against them.

ATTACK TO THE HEAD

The Straight Jab

If a boxer could only perfect one punch it would have to be the jab. It will be the first punch demonstrated by the coach to new pupils entering the gym. A straight jab to the head is thrown with the leading hand and will act as a main point scorer. Working behind a busy solid jab will confuse and throw an opponent off balance giving him less chance to counter-punch. The jab is the industry's punch, helping to create the opportunity to land straight punches with the rear hand, along with hooks and uppercuts with either hand.

When the opponent is within range the attacking boxer will throw his jab with the leading hand, whilst pivoting his body and turning his shoulder. Power will be generated from the drive off his back foot. The leading arm will travel in a straight line rotating the fist just before it makes impact with the palm of the hand facing downwards. Once the leading hand has made contact it must return along the same source to its own guard position. His defending hand must stay close to the side of the head during execution of the jab. There is sometimes the tendency to drop the guard hand when throwing the jab, as it can be easy to forget about one hand when concentrating on the other. It is important to remember that the defending hand is always in place to guard against a counter-attack.

The Straight Right

This punch when thrown from an orthodox stance can be used as a point scorer or a power punch. It will often follow a jab that has measured the distance between an opponent creating openings

The jab, the key to the door that opens the opponent's guard.

The straight right can be used as a point scorer or a power punch.

for a straight right. Explosive power will be driven from the right foot, followed by pivoting of the hips and shoulders leading into an extension of the right arm with the body transferring to the left foot. The right arm is thrown in a straight line, accelerating over the last few inches as with the left jab, twisting the hand just before contact with the palm of the hand facing downwards. Once contact has been made the right hand must quickly return to its defence mode with the left hand in its high guarded position and elbow tucked into the side of the body.

The Left Hook

When executed correctly the left hook can be a devastating punch. For an orthodox boxer, it has the advantage of being a power punch thrown with the hand nearest an opponent. It is an explosive punch that can also be used as a point scorer and is often employed as a counter-punch or as a follow-up to openings created by a jab. As a hook is delivered with a bent arm action its advantage is

The left hook with the palm inwards.

obtained by coming around the outside of an opponent's guard and view. As with all punches, power starts from the feet upwards with the left ankle twisting inwards spinning on the ball of the foot, creating an explosive pivot of the hips and shoulders, transferring body weight from left to right as the arm accelerates towards its target at 45 degrees from the floor. With a basic left hook the palm of the hand faces inwards with the thumb on top. It is important to land the punch with the knuckle part of the glove, or it may be ruled as a slap. Alternatively, it can be thrown with the palm of the glove facing towards the floor. Body weight is transferred to the right side of the body that acts as a door-like hinge and once a punch has landed the body needs to recoil into its defensive position. At all times when the left hook is used the right hand must stay in a high guard position.

The Right Hook

As this punch is thrown with a bent arm action with the rear hand, the feet will need to slide within range, shortening the distance between the boxer and his opponent. Once range has been achieved the right side of the body will pivot, releasing a bent right arm towards its target. This punch like the left hook can land with the palm inwards or downwards. Body weight will switch to the left side of body with the left arm in a high guard position.

The left hook with the palm facing downwards.

aiming upwards. It is often regarded as a close-range punch thrown during in-fighting exchanges, but is equally effective when used at long or mid-range, especially as a counter-punch. Power is generated from legs and hips. When throwing a left uppercut the left shoulder drops with the left arm in a bent, relaxed position with the elbow tucked towards the left hip. A push from the left leg and hip in an explosive thrust drives the attacking arm towards the target, accelerating until impact. As soon as the punch has landed, return the left hand to its guarded position, defending the right arm in a guard position during attack. Boxers should not wind up the uppercut as it will telegraph an attack to their opponent. With a right uppercut the same sequence is used as with the left, but like a right hook the feet will need to shorten distance by stepping in.

The right hook.

The right hook thrown from mid-range.

The Uppercut

Uppercuts can be thrown with either hand to the head and body. It is driven in an exact upright motion keeping it at an angle of 90 degrees. The inside of the glove faces inwards with knuckles

The left uppercut.

The right uppercut.

ATTACK TO THE BODY

The amateur code has often been criticized for not encouraging body punching and focusing on attacks to the head. This, of course, is not the case, but concerns have been aimed towards big competitions where body punching has sometimes been overlooked and has not scored as freely as head punches. It is important to highlight that even if body shots do not catch the eye of the judges as easily as head punches, when landed correctly and with force, a body punch can be the most devastating and sickening punch of all. More often than not a boxer can recover quite quickly from a forceful head blow, but solid punches received to the solar plexus, under the heart or anywhere around the rib area will weaken a boxer making breathing and recovery difficult. A lot of good boxers work to the rule 'kill the body and the head dies in consequence'. This is why body punching must be encouraged and added to the

repertoire of every boxer. Attack to the body will always be more favoured by a smaller, more stockily built boxer, but a taller jab and move style of boxer still needs body-punching techniques included in his arsenal.

The left uppercut to the body.

The right uppercut to the body.

Straight Punches

When throwing a left jab or a straight right to the body, the legs will need to dip, bringing the shoulders level with the target. Obtain power from the rear leg and explosive rotation of the waist, sliding the front foot forward enabling the boxer to be within range before contact. Once the punch has landed, return the hand along the same line with the defending arm maintaining a high guard. A tight solid defence is important as the head will drop in the line of fire of an opponent. It is imperative to use fast footwork in order to move in and out of range.

The straight left to the body.

The straight right to the body.

The Hook

Hooks to the body mostly need to be thrown from close range, therefore a good solid defence has to be practised. When throwing a left hook the chin must be tucked into the left shoulder with the right arm keeping a high guard. Range will be found by sliding in the left front foot with the left shoulder dropping whilst pivoting at the waist and driving power from the legs, hips and shoulders. The left arm will be thrown in a whip-like motion with the palm of the glove facing inwards. The left hand returns to its defence position once impact has been made. To apply the right hook go through the same sequence as for the left, but with a little more drive from the feet to obtain range.

The left hook to the body.

The right hook to the body.

DEFENCE

Covering

It is said that the best form of defence is attack, but every boxer needs to master the 'art of defence' if he is looking for a long career in the sport. There will always come a time for every competitive boxer where he will need to take refuge from a barrage of punches by covering up. There are three basic ways of covering, full cover, half cover and cross-over. A boxer will need to try all three in sparring to find which one is most beneficial to himself, but full cover is usually the guard used by most boxers. At the very first opportunity defending boxers must counter-attack, as staying in a covered position for too long will be seen by a referee as a negative manoeuvre, which could lead to a stoppage.

Full cover.

Half cover.

Cross-over cover.

Blocking

Various forms of blocking punches from an opponent's attacks rate very highly in defensive work. The actual block is a very effective shot

Blocking a straight left with the right hand.

Blocking a straight right with the left hand.

stopper from straight punches to the head. When an attacking boxer throws a straight punch, the defending boxer moves his opposite hand towards the on-coming punch using the palm of the glove to block the shot. A more powerful punch may force the defending glove into his own face, so a small backward step once the punch has been blocked will distance the defending glove from the boxer. Once the boxer has blocked an attack with one hand he will now be in a position to counter with his opposite hand, which has been in a high guard position during the attack launched by his opponent.

Shoulder Block

This is a form of defence against a straight right to the head. The attacking blow is blocked by the left shoulder and forearm, which are both raised and kept close together. Body weight is transferred to the right leg with the chin tightly tucked into the left shoulder. A counter-punch can be thrown by the right hand, which is held in a high defensive guard.

The shoulder block against a straight right.

The wedge block against a straight right.

The forearm block against a right hook.

Glove Block

This is used to defend against an uppercut to the head. When a right uppercut is thrown the defending boxer uses the palm of his right glove to block the opponent's strike. Against a left uppercut, the defending boxer will block with his left glove. Care must be observed towards the opponent's free hand, as the defending boxer will have left a gap between his guard and the attacking boxer's guarding hand.

Wedge Block

This is a defensive move that is an effective block against straight punches and hooks. The defending arm moves rapidly inside the opponent's advancing blow forming a wedge between the elbow. Just before contact is made the defending arm flexes, presenting a solid resistance. The opposite hand is kept in a relaxed defensive guard ready to counter.

Forearm Block

This is a good defensive move against hooks, which brings the shoulder inside an attacking punch by pivoting the hips. The defending hand will move high towards the forehead using shoulders and forearms for the block. Turning the shoulder will give extra leverage for a counter with the opposite hand.

The glove block against a right uppercut.

The elbow block against a right hook to the body.

The inside wedge against a straight right to the body.

Elbow Block

This is used as a defence against hooks and upper-cuts to the body, keeping arms tight into the body whilst pivoting at the waist. Against punches thrown with the left arm the defending boxer twists to his left, against a right punch he will twist to his right. Elbows are tucked in, absorbing punches with the elbows and forearms. Both hands are held close to the chin ready to counter with either hand.

Inside Wedge

These block attacks to the body by quickly dropping the opposite arm to the attacking arm in a sweeping motion. The forearm is flexed as contact is made on the opponent's wrist or glove. The opposite arm is kept in its guard position for a counter.

Outside and Inside Parry

The outside parry is an effective defence against straight punches to the head, taking a defending boxer outside his opponent's attack. Against a left jab to the head a defending boxer will make contact with the inside of his right glove on the wrist and forearm of his opponent's left arm. The same manoeuvre is used in defence of a straight right to the head by parrying with the left hand. An inside parry to a left jab to the head is used by moving inside the attacking boxer's left arm and parrying with the outside of the right glove. Caution has to be taken when using this tactic as it will leave the defending boxer's head in the line of his opponent's right hand. Parrying straight punches to the body are a similar action to an inside wedge. When defending a left jab to the body with an outside parry the left arm sweeps

Outside parry against a straight left.

Outside parry against a straight right.

Inside parry against a straight left.

Outside parry against a straight right to the body, with the defending boxer sliding his front foot to the left.

downwards, making contact with the palm of the left glove against the opponent's left wrist. The same arm action takes place with an outside parry to a straight right to the body with the defending boxer using the inside of the right glove to deflect the punch. A slight step with the front foot will move the defending boxer outside his opponent's right hand. Inside parries are another alternative to defending a left jab to the body by contacting an attacking blow with the inside of the right glove.

With all parrying, the defending arm must stay in its position and be ready to counter.

The Lay Back

Transferring the body weight towards the rear foot will bring a defending boxer out of range from any attacking strike. As an opponent attacks, the boxer leans back without moving his feet, bending the back leg whilst keeping the front leg relatively straight with the knee soft and relaxed. Once an opponent has committed to the attack a counter can be launched from either hand, with an explosive push from the rear foot.

Push Away

Unlike the lay back it will be footwork that moves a defending boxer out of range from his opponent's attack. As an advancing punch approaches, the boxer pushes back from his front foot as his rear foot leads, keeping arms in a high guard position. Counters can also come from either hand and a powerful push from the rear foot.

The push away against a straight left to the head.

As the attacking boxer leads, the defending boxer pushes off his front foot as his back foot leads.

The lay back against a straight left to the head.

Slipping Outside and Inside

All boxers need a good head movement, which enables them to slip and roll punches. Slipping an oncoming strike requires a slight movement of the head, bringing it out of line from straight punches. When slipping outside an attacking left jab the body quickly transfers weight to the right side, whilst dropping the right shoulder as the opponent's punch slips over the left shoulder. Against a straight right to the head, the same motion is used as for a left jab, but slipping to the left. Slipping inside is a far more risky manoeuvre, as it will bring a defending boxer inside his opponent's defence. To slip a jab, body weight moves to the left while the left shoulder drops. Both hands need to be high on guard, as the boxer will be in the line of his opponent's right hand. To slip inside against

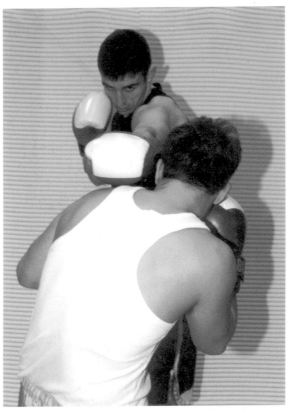

Slipping outside a straight left.

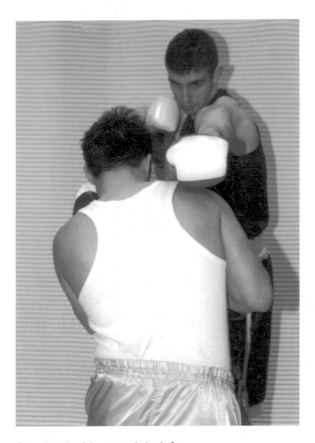

Slipping inside a straight left.

Slipping outside a straight right.

a right hand will be as for defending the left jab but slipping to the right. Tight defence is vital when slipping inside, and counter-punches can come from either hand. As an addition to slipping, lateral footwork such as 'stepping across' will move the defending boxer outside his opponent's attack. Also it will put him in a good position for a counter outside an opponent's guard.

Ducking

Quickly dropping the body with an increased bend of the knees will take the boxer below oncoming straight punches and hooks. It is important that hands are held high and the head does not drop below the opponent's belt, as this will be seen as a dangerous use of the head by the referee. Counter-punches to the body can come from either hand.

Rolling

As with ducking, rolling will move the head below an advancing punch. As a straight punch or hook approaches the head the boxer rolls inside, under

Rolling. The defending boxer starts to roll in a clockwise direction against the opponent's right hook.

The defending boxer's head drops below the oncoming strike.

Ducking under a straight left to the head. This puts the defending boxer in a good position to counter to the body with either hand.

The defending boxer comes outside the opponent's defence. This will put him in a good position to counter with the left hook.

Head Movement

On the final point on defence, it is important to reiterate how vital head movement is. Obviously head movement is used when slipping and rolling punches, but the head needs to be moving constantly. The wearing of headguards sometimes gives a boxer a false sense of security, as they feel the head is well protected and guarded. Any punch landed with force on the target area of the head will score and can cause damage, even when wearing a headguard. A boxer has to instinctively try to avoid punches as he sees them coming. He also has to anticipate and discourage being punched, by applying constant head movement. A boxer must always remember that a static head makes for an easy target.

and finally outside the strike. Hands are held high on guard, and once outside the attacking punch the defending boxer is well positioned to counter.

CHAPTER 3
Advanced Techniques

Ringcraft

As a contact sport, boxing is very complex and every ounce of physical strength has to be called upon. Not only does a boxer need to outmanoeuvre his opponent but he will also have to out-think him. Boxing is a physical chess game where each participant looks for openings to make his move.

All good coaches will teach their boxers the skill of ring craft to enable them to grasp the importance of techniques required within a boxing ring. Skills such as footwork, to quickly change direction and the ability to deliver punches from various angles, or the art of cutting down the ring deterring an opponent from moving freely are essential. Different styles create different contests and tactics are always important, but many boxers will know little or nothing of their opponent's style until the first bell sounds. This is why a variety of tactics need to be practised in preparation for various opponents.

Some boxers may dictate the pace, others will demand the centre of the ring, while hit and move will be another's game plan. Every boxer will need to find his own rhythm and keep his composure allowing him to control the tempo of a bout, but it is also important to remember that he must possess the ability and skill to alter his strategy should his opponent's tactics break that rhythm. A boxer who is conversant with ring craft and utilizes those techniques that he has been taught and makes optimal use of them, will mostly be victorious.

Footwork

A vast variety of footwork is an integral part of any boxer's success, and failure to realize this fact will leave him with very limited ability. Boxers need to change directions in a bout and not just in straight lines. A quick step off to the side, either leading with the left or right foot, can be utilized for evasion or as an attacking manoeuvre allowing punches to be thrown from various angles outside an opponent's defence. Lateral footwork, such as sidestepping an opponent by leading with the right foot whilst also transferring bodyweight to the right side, will bring the boxer outside the left hand of his opponent's guard allowing good leverage on his punches. Moving to the outside of an opponent's right hand with a step off with the left foot is just as effective, allowing punches to head and body from an outside position.

The switch step, which is a variation of the side step, is a skilful move that will take a boxer outside the left arm of an opponent's defence. For an orthodox boxer it can be an evasive move against a straight left or as a quick-shift change of

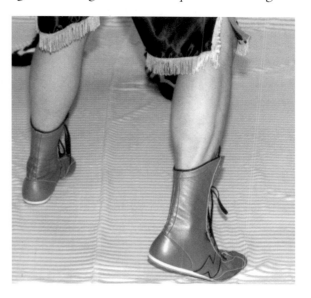

The side step to the right.

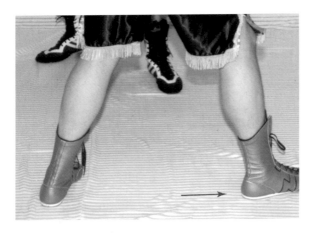

This will move the boxer outside the opponent's guard.

direction to allow him to throw punches from angles outside an opponent's view. The switch step is performed by sliding the front leg towards the rear leg whilst simultaneously sliding the rear leg outwards, bringing the feet out of line of an opponent, whilst then bringing the front leg forwards outside the opponent's left guard. This lateral footwork manoeuvre will put a boxer in a position outside the line of attack of his opponent and punches such as left or right crosses or right hooks to the head can be launched.

Gliding movements to the left or right will not only take a boxer trapped on the ropes out of the line of an attack, but can also be an advantage as an attacking move. Like side-stepping, the boxer can put himself in a position to attack at an angle outside his opponent's guard.

The glide to the right.

The glide to the right or left will take the boxer out of the line of attack and into a good position to counter.

When moving to the right using the glide the boxer spins off the ball of his left foot towards the right, while bringing his right foot outwards outside his opponent's left hand. Gliding to the left again will have the boxer spinning off his front foot towards the left, followed by his right leg. Again, advantage is gained from attacking from the outside of the advancing or defending opposition.

Variations of Punches

By having a wide variety of punches a boxer gives himself more ammunition in his armoury, preparing him for any situation. Jabs for example are the bread and butter punch for all boxers, but there is nothing in the rules that states that they have to be thrown directly in front of an opponent. As already covered, lateral footwork will position a boxer to punch at an angle, which will not only slip him outside an opponent's attack but also leave his opponent in no position to get any purchase on his own shots. Any punch can be used from outside an opponent to body or head and over or under the defending boxer's guard. Sometimes being unorthodox can work as an important ploy to a boxer's game plan and improvisation is important. If a punch lands on its target with the knuckle part of the glove it will score. Punches do not have to be thrown in a conventional style as long as they land cleanly, such as straight punches and hooks that which can be launched in a slightly upwards or over action inside or outside an opponent's guard.

A boxer must find his range when launching an attack with his distance varying from short, medium and long range. A shorter stockier-type boxer will tend to use his short levers to connect with power punches such as hooks and uppercuts on the inside. Taller boxers with long levers will generally whip in his punches from long range, taking advantage of the distance between him and his opponent. For a rangy orthodox boxer long-range left hooks and uppercuts are useful attacks, which will often take an opponent out of his stride. Punching off the left jab is another

The long-range left hook. The hook, like all punches, can be thrown from long, medium or short range.

A variation of the left hook, used as a counter-punch against a straight right to the head.

The right hand over the top. Note the curve in the arm.

technique that can unsettle the opposition and is favourable against counter-punches. A hook off a jab or uppercut off a jab will delay an opponent's time to counter and can totally throw him off guard as a second punch will be coming around or through his defence. As the jab should have forced the defending boxer backwards the attacking boxer will need to step in with his second punch. A double jab is equally effective and will disorientate an opponent as the second jab has to be thrown quickly and while moving in.

For orthodox boxers a variation to the right, is the right hand over the top. This is a power shot that travels in an up and over motion, aiming down towards the opposition's chin. The right shoulder and fist rotate as much as possible with the chin tucked into the right shoulder.

Combination Punching

Once the boxer is proficient at throwing single punches he will then need to be taught how to launch an attack with a cluster of punches known as combination punching. A combination is two or more punches thrown in one single attack. The first combination taught by a coach to an orthodox boxer will nearly always be a left and right to the head or to a southpaw the right and left to the head. This is often referred to as the 'old one-two', but from those two punches a whole selection of various combinations to the head and body can be taught. Once he has become more accomplished at using combinations, the boxer can then test them out during sparring sessions. Footwork is vital as the feet will slide an attacking boxer within striking distance to land each punch, while keeping well balanced to allow a free flow of punches. The non-punching hand must always be held in a high guard position in readiness to defend against an opponent's counter. Feet will need to get out of range quickly once a sequence of punches has been launched. Speed and timing are essential when using combination punching. There are many and varied combinations and it is the decision of the boxer which one he favours and in which order. Most coaches will teach their charges to throw combinations in sequence of threes and fives starting and finishing with his leading hand. This closes down the target of the attacking boxer and will not leave him square on to his opponent's counter-punches. Below are a selection of combination punches for an orthodox boxer. To apply these techniques to a southpaw stance, the boxer will need to mirror-image each punch.

Two-Punch Combination

1. Left jab – straight right to head
2. Left jab – right hook to head
3. Left jab – right uppercut to head

4. Double left jab to head
5. Left jab – left hook to head
6. Left jab – left uppercut to head
7. a) Jab to body – jab to head
   b) Jab to head – jab to body

8. a) Left hook to body – left hook to head
   b) Left hook to head – left hook to body

9. Straight right – left hook to head
10. Straight right – left uppercut to head

The one-two combination. The straight left to the head...

...followed by the straight right to the head.

Three-Punch Combination

1. Left jab – straight right – straight left to head
2. Left jab – straight right – left hook to head
3. Left jab – straight right – left uppercut to head
4. Left hook to body – left hook – straight right to head
5. Left hook to body – left hook – right hook to head
6. Left hook to body – left hook – right uppercut to head
7. Right hook to body – right hook – left hook to head
8. Right hook to body – right hook – left uppercut to head
9. Straight right to body – straight right – left hook to head
10. Straight right to body – straight right – left uppercut to head

A three-punch combination. Left hook to the body...

...left hook to the head...

...straight right to the head.

Punches can be added as can the sequence of punches be altered, since the variation of combinations are endless. In amateur boxing any cluster of five or more blows landing unanswered against a defending boxer will almost certainly force the referee to award a standing count against him.

Counter–Punching

After every successful defensive action against an attack the defending boxer can score with his own counter-punch. The defensive strategy that a boxer uses will dictate which punch or punches he will counter with. For example, a right-handed block or parry to a left jab could be countered with the defending boxer's own left jab. The optimum

A counter against a straight left to the head, by ducking below the punch and countering with a straight right to the body.

The boxer on the left blocks the attacking left jab with his right hand and counters with his left hand.

The boxer on the right slips inside the attacking left arm and counters with a left uppercut.

The counter-attack with the boxer on the left landing his punch first.

various opposition. A counter-attack is a speedy reply to an attacking punch. As the attacking boxer strikes, the defending boxer launches his own attack against his opponent's lead, beating him to the punch.

Boxing off the Ropes

A coach will usually advise his boxer not to get himself trapped on the ropes, as once under attack movement for evasion is limited. Some boxers use the ropes to help draw their opponent in for a counter-attack. Lateral movement such as side steps and the glide as covered in the footwork section are effective defensive moves, bringing the defending boxer off the ropes and into a position to counter. Turning an opponent will also take the defender out of the line of attack. Once the opponent is in close, the orthodox boxer pulls his opponent's left elbow with the palm of his right glove. As he palms the oncoming boxer's elbow he simultaneously steps to the right and away off the

hand to counter with will usually be the guarding hand and not the one defending the punch. Speed and timing are important factors for a successful counter, enabling a defending boxer to take advantage of openings created by his opponent's attack. A counter will need to be well-timed and carried out with speed. Single blows and combinations can be thrown off a counter to head and body and a variety of counters may be needed against

A boxer requires good defence and evasive ability to box off the ropes.

ropes. The pull needs to be fast and forceful to turn the opponent and throw him off balance, with the guarding left hand held in a high position in defence against the attacker's right hand. Turning an opponent whilst in-fighting can also be employed.

If the defending boxer is trapped against the ropes or in a corner, he must stay well covered protecting his head and body. It is important when under a barrage of punches that the defending boxer should not take his eyes off his opponent. Once he cannot see what punches are coming towards him he will find it very difficult to get off the ropes or throw any counter-punches. If the defending boxer cannot manoeuvre himself off the ropes or out of the corner, he will need to try to grab or hold his opponent before the referee steps in.

Turning an opponent to get off the ropes or to get away from boxing at close quarters.

Variations of Style

A boxer may possess all the attributes needed to succeed in competition, but he may be pitted against someone so unorthodox and with limited ability that they are effectively awkward and bring the more gifted boxer down a level. A boxer who may not be blessed with natural skill will work to his own strengths. He might have to rely on spoiling tactics such as holding and leaning on his opponent to break down his composure and rhythm. This type of opposition totally frustrates the better boxer who relies on quick movement and agility. Any competitor reverting to spoiling tactics will still need to be seen working and landing punches as any method used to stop the flow of a bout will result in a warning or even a disqualification by the referee. Styles make bouts and a clash of styles such as two defensively minded boxers competing against one another can result in a very dull contest.

The classic bout is often between a boxer and a fighter (The Matador v The Bull). There will never be a favourite in this encounter if both boxers are equal in ability. The boxer will compete in an upright style with his weight towards his back foot. This creates even more distance between a taller boxer and a usually smaller, stockier fighter. To beat the fighter, the boxer will be aiming to score points with his jab and his long-range punches. He will attempt to move in and out of range to land his shots quickly, retreating away from his opponent's counters. The boxer will tend to rely on speed and accuracy to keep his opponent at bay and will not want to be involved in boxing at close quarters with someone who may be physically stronger. A boxer may choose to box on the back foot, scoring with snappy fast jabs against the oncoming fighter.

The fighter comes forwards using plenty of head movement in a bobbing and weaving style. He must attempt to break the distance, getting inside the boxer's long-range punches and inside his defence. The fighter's body weight will tend to be towards the front foot and he will often be a counter-puncher. It is rare that a fighter will outjab a boxer, so he must close the range, working behind shorter punches to the head and body.

The taller boxer will always want to keep at long range against a small boxer.

Against a constantly moving boxer he might select to dominate the centre of the ring or cut off the ring, driving his opponent into a corner or against the ropes.

In-Fighting

Boxing on the inside will always be best adopted by a shorter, stockier style of boxer who can gain an advantage over a taller opponent by working at close quarters. Breaking down the distance to obtain that inside position will be one of the main problems that he must overcome. To shorten the distance, speedy direct footwork will be vital whilst evading his opponent's attack. A tight tucked-in defence will be essential, making himself an elusive small target. Once inside his opponent's defence various short-range punches can be thrown in clusters to the head and body. Due to the close range it is difficult to obtain good leverage on the punches, so a powerful pivot of the trunk of the body will be necessary. Feet will be positioned in a more square-on stance than normal, but a solid depth in base must be obtained to keep a good balance.

Close-quarter exchanges are often fast and competitive and the boxer who sustains most of the blows will often try to grab and hold to gain respite from the onslaught of punches. Referees will warn a boxer for holding too much but once

The smaller boxer will look to try and work inside.

In-fighting requires great physical strength and fitness to sustain pressure on the opponent.

there is a clinch between two boxers the referee will call 'break'. This will lose an advantage gained from the boxer winning the exchange.

Once an exchange on the inside breaks down, the movement away from an opponent has to be carried out with caution. This is because moving back from a square-on stance could leave the boxer exposed and open to an attack. So a high guard with chin tucked into the shoulders must be kept during the break away.

Every boxer will have to learn to fight on the inside as even the most accomplished tall, rangy boxer may come up against someone so strong and forceful that they cannot always keep him at bay with long-range punches. A top boxer will possess the ability to be a 'box fighter'; this is when a boxer can box at range or go 'toe to toe', fighting in close if he needs to.

Feinting

Boxing is a skill sport where a boxer needs to use his mental awareness as well as his physical strength. Once basic footwork and defensive tactics have been mastered, skills to disorientate opponents will need to be developed. Skills such as feinting can cause confusion and create openings for an attack. The feint gives an impression of moving in one direction or throwing a certain punch that forces the opposition to defend against attacks he believes are being launched. The whole body can be used when feinting, such as slightly stepping to the left then quickly switching attack to the right. Also showing a left arm as if to throw a jab then changing the direction of the punch into a hook or uppercut. A change of punch, like feinting with the right arm and launching a left-arm punch, can also be effective as can feinting an attack from body to head or head to body.

Drawing

The practice of drawing an opponent is an art used by the most skilful of boxers. Its aim is to draw an opponent into an attack, leaving openings

in his guard. To achieve this the boxer has to present gaps in his own defence such as dropping his arm or leaving a gap between his guard. This will show the opposing boxer a target, inviting him to attack. Keeping the right distance is essential, as to be too far out of range will not draw the opponent in and too close within range could be dangerous, as the boxer could be a victim of his own deception.

Reaction speed is vital as a split-second delay could be costly. This is a very advanced skill where speed, timing and distance have to be precise. Feinting and drawing are abilities that will confuse and frustrate opponents and a frustrated boxer is usually a beaten boxer. Both skills need to be practised in the gym and perfected before attempting them in contests.

A boxer can draw his opponent into an attack, by leaving himself open inviting his opponent to commit himself. The defending boxer can then launch a counter-attack.

The Orthodox v The Southpaw

Most boxers have the tendency to move in the direction of their leading hand and in the case of the orthodox against the southpaw this should be advisable, as it brings each boxer away from his opponent's danger punch. But as with any style of opposition, direction and movement must vary and not be predictable as an opponent may possess equal power in either hand. For most orthodox boxers the southpaw often proves to be a very awkward proposition, as both leading hand and front foot are unnaturally close to one another. Both boxers when using the leading hand will find it 'beneficial' if the punch is delivered outside the vision of the opponent. Jabs and hooks thrown around the opposition's leading hand and line of vision will be effective as a lead or counter-punch. Strikes aimed through the middle of the defensive guard with the traditionally stronger punching rear hand are also favoured by both styles. Bouts between the right-handed and left-handed opponent can often be cagey affairs, with the boxer who is more proficient in lateral movement, switching attack and counter-punching often coming out on top.

The orthodox boxer will try to bring his leading left hand around the southpaw guard.

A straight right through the middle of the southpaw guard is also another favoured attack.

The southpaw boxer often works off the counter, slipping inside and outside the opponent's defences and attacking with counters to the head...

...and counters to the body.

CHAPTER 4

The Role of the Coach

Behind every successful amateur boxing club is a small group of coaches who give their spare time towards maintaining the club's success. It is these men who spot early potential in the youngsters and help convert raw talent and energy into technical ability and controlled aggression. There are many clubs that are self-sufficient and often housed in run-down buildings with very little funding. The coach will not only have to produce an accomplished team of boxers, but he will need to keep a roof over their heads as well. The larger, more established clubs will have a secretary and a treasurer and may even have sponsorship. This will relieve the coach of any added pressure, thus allowing them time to concentrate on the important job of training the squad. Even if he has a good backroom staff it will be the head coach who is responsible for the overall running of the club and when he is not in the gym he will be arranging matches for his club members.

England has four levels of coaching, assistant ABA Coach Part 1, full ABA Coach Part 2, senior coach and advanced coach. Coaches must be at least assistant level to work in an amateur boxing club or second a contest. Although not a necessity it is an advantage to have someone in the corner who has experienced the nervous tension, and sometimes even the fear, that every boxer encounters when competing. Having a good coach in the corner is vastly important to the boxer, as he will need to assess each round of his boxer's performance, gauging his strengths and weaknesses. There is only a one-minute rest in between rounds and the boxer may be overawed and tired, but the corner-man has to gain his full attention, making sure that what is being told to his boxer is being taken on board. The second will be required to talk clearly and precisely, staying cool under pressure and in total command. He will be the sole man permitted into the ring with his boxer at the end of the round, with his assistant passing up the water bottle or spray and towel, whilst rinsing out the gumshield. During each break, the coach who is in the ring should be the only one giving out instructions, as commands from his assistant second will only confuse the boxer. During the rounds the coach himself should stay calm and must not instruct from outside the ring, as this will result in a warning and if it continues he will be ordered away from the ring. In this situation the assistant coach will take over as chief second. Emotions can run high but a good corner man must not let them cloud his judgement. If he feels his boxer is taking too much punishment then he has to pull him out of the bout. This he can do by throwing the towel into the ring to attract the referee's attention. The proud boxer will hate being pulled out by his corner but his safety will always be the coach's number one priority. Some naturally gifted boxers who enter into coaching can sometimes find difficulty accepting that the boxer he is training may not possess the ability he once had and may struggle to understand that what came easy to him, may not come so easy for someone else. A good balance must be found, as a coach could be technically brilliant but have little patience and poor communication skills. So he must nurture each of his charges individually, assessing his strengths and weaknesses. Some boxers may struggle with self-belief and require a few motivational words of support while another can overestimate his own ability, crossing the line between confidence and arrogance. This boxer would need to be brought down to reality but without having his aspirations shattered.

Micky Redman, twenty-five years an ABA coach.

It is the skill of these people, which makes successful coaches. Every gym will have its fair share of youngsters who will attend each session and train as hard or even harder than anyone else, but lack what is needed to be a competitive boxer. The coach's responsibility is to assess the ability of the youngsters and he will be the one who breaks the news that he is not good enough to compete. As much as he may desire to do so, it would be irresponsible of him to put a boxer into the ring if he felt he was not good enough.

Coaching the Successful Boxer

The training programme that the coach devises for his boxers needs to be structured, aiming towards increased development in physical fitness and technique. He has to be familiar with the latest training trends whilst balancing them with older tried and tested methods. A good knowledge of nutrition is important as diet and weight play a major role in a boxer's life.

Most amateur clubs will have at least three trainers within its gym, allowing time for the head coach to work with his more senior boxers while the assistant coaches can concentrate on newcomers and novices. The senior coach has to oversee the training of every person in his club from schoolboys to seniors, but he is judged by his boxers and the more success they achieve the more successful the club becomes. A boxer must have complete trust and faith in his coach's judgement, as the coach is the person who will matchmake for the boxer. If he were to overmatch his boxer and he were badly beaten that responsibility would lie with the coach. In championship bouts that burden is taken away from him, but it takes a lot of work and sacrifices to get the boxer to that level. Since the introduction of the novice championships it has made it a lot easier for a boxer to gain championship experience. The novice championships category A is for boxers who have had under ten bouts, category B is for under twenty bouts. This will prove a major foundation and testing ground when preparing a boy for a full ABA Championship.

A boy's education of the sport starts the moment he enters the gym. If a coach can spot that he has the basic talent and drive to compete, he will then be provided with a high-performance conditioning programme. Once he has shown aptitude for training and has acquired the basic fitness required, an intensive routine of technical skill and ability training will be added. One of the most efficient ways of teaching and improving techniques is through the practice of pad work. Being a competent pad man is one of the most important roles that a coach will perform in the gym. Pad work will not only develop punching power and accuracy but it will also act as a good source for improving footwork and movement while increasing the ability to master the more advanced skills. The hook and jab pads as they are known, are the ideal way of practising timing and speed combinations, with the coach calling out various instructions whilst providing a moving

A national coach with the England squad during the 1980s, the late Dennis Jackson uses his skill in the corner during an international tournament.

target. These sessions provide the coach with the opportunity to teach on a one-to-one basis, allowing him to assess technique and analyse any faults.

Another method that is very instrumental in advanced pad work is the introduction of coach spar pads. These are target pads that are shaped in the same form as a boxing glove. For the coach this is an excellent tool that allows him to correct any specific flaw in a defence. This he can do by throwing light punches towards the target, exposing any gaps or holes in the guard. This schools a boxer into punching, moving and defending, as with traditional hook and jab pads there may be a tendency to stay within range once throwing a punch. After launching a punch towards the coach spar pad a counter is always imminent, thus forcing the boxer to speed up his reactions towards his defence and movement from in and out of range. Also it will act as a reminder to break any bad habits that he may be forming.

Another piece of equipment that is a useful aid to the trainer is the body protector. This is a well-padded guard that is worn by the coach, allowing his boxer to practise body shots. It will also help him to gain confidence to slip in and out of the guard whilst attempting to land punches upon the mid-section.

Sparring

An experienced coach will always treat the introduction of new boxers to sparring with caution, as to expose a raw novice to an open sparring session too early in his development could potentially lose his club a promising prospect. The aspiring boxer may possess all the attributes to succeed, such as physique, balance, co-ordination, fitness and strength, but until he has been tested in sparring a coach cannot really assess his competitive desire. If he has been worked on the coach spar pads he will have had some experience of slipping and defending against light punches, thus improving his evasion skills. This will be a totally different scenario from actually sparring and early sessions will have to be very controlled with the emphasis on technique. Touch or tag sparring is usually the most effective method of teaching newcomers the art of control, as punches are aimed towards the target area but reduced in speed and force. Sessions must be structured around tactics and technique and it has to be stressed that although punches are aimed at one another they must be thrown without force. Technique sparring is an opportunity for both boxers to put into practice all they have been taught in the gym.

The key word is control, and by setting a range of various themes for the participants to follow, it will help take away any competitive edge. Anyone entering the ring for the first time will often feel that he has to perform to gain the approval of his coach. This adds unnecessary pressure on the boxer and along with the nerves and anticipation usually results in the sparring session turning into a brawl. Nothing is learnt or gained by this, except how *not* to approach a contest. All the technical boxing that has been taught over the past months in the gym is totally forgotten. To put both boxers at ease during these early encounters in the ring, the coach must stress that it is *technical sparring* that should be the first type of sparring the novice boxer attempts. This form of sparring is totally structured to teach a boxer the skills and techniques that he will need for competition. Various attacking and defending moves will be practised between the two boxers as the coach keeps a tight control on the speed of movement whilst ensuring that the power of punches is totally reduced. One specific technique should be practised at a time, with each boxer changing roles from attacking to defending. As each boxer grasps the fundamentals of the technique session and grows in confidence, speed and movement may be increased. The next step up is *condition sparring*, which is when the coach sets various themes for each boxer to follow to teach them skills and techniques. Speed of movement will be at actual pace with power still decreased. Themes that could be set may include only using the jab or one boxer attacking as his partner defends. Coaches must take time to ensure that each participant understands the conditions he has set and observes them fully. This style of sparring helps the boxer to settle into having a live opponent in front of him, but without too much added pressure. Not only will he learn from this but it will also gain him a lot more confidence.

As a boxer becomes more conditioned and comfortable in light sparring he will then need to step up into *open sparring*. This will be the closest he will come to actual competition, but it must always be treated as a spar. Speed and pace will increase and force will be added to punches, but open sparring should be worked at no more than 90 per cent of competition level. Hard sparring is essential while preparing to compete and punches are thrown with more power, but intent to hurt a sparring partner must never be encouraged, although anyone who has ambitions of competing needs to experience the feeling of receiving a hurtful punch, as he and his coach can gauge his reactions and his punch resistance. Once open sparring has been introduced into the developing boxer's routine, it allows the coach opportunity to assess his temperament. Newcomers to sparring will be carefully watched to see how they cope once they have been hit by a forceful blow, with a receptive coach monitoring how they respond. Will the boxer whilst sustaining increased pressure or getting caught reset himself while quickly regaining his composure, or will he be totally disoriented and panic? These are questions that must be answered way before anybody enters the ring to compete.

No training routine carried out in the gym can replace sparring, as it is the only real way of assessing the prospect's ability and fitness. Some coaches will have their club members sparring as often as possible while others may restrict sessions believing that too much sparring can cause a boxer to become stale and jaded with a risk of injuries. It can be true that a boxer can leave all his best work back in the gym. While looking accomplished and relaxed in the comfort of his own club he may often fail to perform to the best of his ability in competition. Every boxing club may have its own methods of training to try to achieve the most effective way to help their team become successful, but it cannot be emphasized enough how essential sparring is. It is just finding the correct balance between too much and not enough. During sparring the headguard and gumshield must be worn at all times and it is advisable also to wear a foul protector. Gloves for seniors will vary between 14oz and 16oz depending on the weight category. For competition all gloves worn are 10oz, so it can be an advantage to have boxers who are preparing for their first contest, sparring a few rounds in contest gloves. Anyone who gets caught with a punch from a lighter glove for the first time may find it quite a shock. Newcomers to competition do need to experience how much lighter the 10oz gloves feel in comparison to the larger glove that

Sparring, the boxer's first real test.

In a busy gym, group technical sparring can be organized.

they will have used in the gym. Although the hands will feel lighter and faster, there is also a sense of the head being a bigger target as the smaller glove, obviously, does not cover and defend as much as the larger gloves. Of course, this will also apply to the opposition as he, too, will be wearing smaller gloves. Sparring in 10oz gloves is a way of preparing the novice boxer for his first bout, but it should not be practised too often. Communication between the boxer and coach has to be maintained at all times by having regular meetings with members of the club. Talks should be built around tactics, techniques, fault finding and building confidence and motivation. Every club member will look towards his head coach for inspiration and will rely on him to rectify any individual mistakes and obtain improvements. Visual aids are useful in keeping the group attentive and focused. Video footage of team members sparring can be extremely helpful when pinpointing individual faults and errors whilst also highlighting good and positive aspects of each boxer's performance. This will also give the boxer the opportunity to see for himself any faults he may or may not have made and with the support of his coach be able to rectify.

Coaching Children

Many children from the age of nine upwards join their local boxing club with aspirations of becoming a competitive boxer. Unfortunately only a few will possess the ability to represent their team and because of a lack of facilities and resources, many clubs will let go youngsters who are not likely to reach competition level. Some children may be late developers and in future years could play an important role within the club. Even if they never reach contest standard, children can acquire so much from boxing training, gaining improved fitness and strength, learning a new skill and, above all, gaining confidence. Training children has to be disciplined, but it also has to be fun. Children do often require lots of attention, which in most busy clubs is not practical, so a structured programme needs to be set for them. Patience is essential as some may not grasp certain

Coaching children needs to be basic and fun.

aspects of the programme as quickly as others. They can also become bored quickly, so the technique taught needs to be very basic. Routines should be simple with plenty of variation including bag and pad work with skipping. During shadow boxing children have the tendency to lose interest and switch off as they are not actually punching anything and can find it difficult to imagine an opponent in front of them. One way of getting them to respond to this important part of the boxing training routine, is to pair each of them with a partner. Having two youngsters facing each other during shadow boxing will give them the feeling of facing an opponent. While they are not actually making any contact with each other, they use the practice to look for openings and how to slip punches. Non-contact sparring can be demonstrated in the same way by both children wearing gloves, but only simulating the sparring again with no contact being made. This will help with the development of the youngsters' technical ability while teaching them the skills of the sport. When possible, whilst training children new to boxing, a fun element can be introduced to help relax newcomers into what can be quite a demanding training environment. If time and space allow, the use of fun circuit programmes, which still involve boxing techniques, is a way of teaching children the fundamentals of boxing whilst making it enjoyable.

Coaching the competitive schoolboy is an entirely different prospect from coaching the competitive senior. The novice schoolboy boxer will need to keep his boxing simple and training him should be kept basic. Advanced techniques and clever footwork will be too much for a young mind to absorb. Simple straight punches, defence manoeuvres and footwork are all they will need when introducing them to competitive boxing. As they progress so will their technique, with the better young prospects entering the junior and cadet championships.

The Making of a Champion

Every boxing trainer hopes that one day a young boy will walk into his gym with all the natural ability and attributes of a certain future champion. Of course this can be a rare occurrence, as many coaches have dedicated their lives to boxing without ever producing that special boxer. There will be just as many coaches who have had that boy come to their club looking certain to succeed, only to be left disappointed. After months or even years of nurturing and schooling this future star, he gives up the sport and gives into the needs of being a teenager. This to a coach can be heartbreaking after all the hard work he has put in, but for the sake of all his other club members he has to put it down to experience.

Promising youngsters who leave the sport, often return some years later when they feel mature enough to commit to training and compete. The pressure of training at any level is very hard on any young boxer and if a boy has been singled out as a future star, they can often find it hard to deal with. Many boys who return to boxing as young men, often find they are better equipped to handle the discipline they need to achieve success in the sport.

Every boxer who enters the ring to compete is in his own way special, but to become a successful champion he must possess many attributes, some of which he is born with and others that he can perfect through hard work and dedication. Getting into the right mind-set is one of the first components a boxer requires. Any experienced coach will have at some time had to suffer the frustration of having a gifted boxer in his club, who possesses all the physical attributes to becoming a champion, but unfortunately has a poor attitude. For some boxers as with all gifted sports people, everything appears to come very easily to them. This can sometimes make them complacent, especially in their training.

A true champion will always put the hours in the gym and keep his disciplined lifestyle throughout the competitive season. Cheating in training and with nutrition will eventually catch up with a boxer, as everyone is capable of getting beaten. Many champions who may not have been blessed with natural skills and ability have succeeded through hard work, desire and dedication. It is usually found that the boxer who wants it the most will have his arm raised at the end of the bout. A major factor behind the Cuban and Russian dominance in amateur boxing throughout the world is their self-belief. From an early age it is instilled in their minds that they are winners. Outthinking an opponent has always played an important role in amateur boxing and since the introduction of computer and scoring machines, emphasis is even more on technical ability. Knockouts are very rare in the amateur sport as most bouts are won on points that can only be awarded for landing punches on the target area with sufficient force. The original score card judging allowed a judge more of an individual preference to his scoring. The favoured boxer would score twenty points per round and would not only be scored on punches landed, but points would be awarded for skill, style, workrate and defensive work. This of course left room for debate, as each judge would have their own preference for a particular style of boxer.

If the boxer can stop his opponent all well and good, but with the scoring system the boxer has to focus on scoring with clean single shots that will register on the scoring machine. It must be remembered that the machines are still operated by the judges, so they must see the punch land. Many Eastern Europeans adopted a style of boxing with their leading hand outstretched, constantly moving and probing for openings to land with the leading hand, whilst also trying to draw the opponent on to the stronger back hand. Coaches world-wide have now introduced this style to many of their boxers. More and more coaches have converted orthodox boxers into southpaws, which favours the counter-punching style that can be beneficial in the point-scoring system.

Coaches, like the boxers, must have an open mind to new ideas and styles; it does not matter how experienced the coach is, he should always be open to fresh ideas. Boxers can always go through periods when nothing is going to plan inside the ring and when this happens the coach will be called upon to work with his boxer, trying out new techniques to address the problem.

There is no such thing as a perfect boxer, as every boxer will have a fault of some kind. It is the coach's role to try to get all of his boxers to fulfil their potential. If he has a boxer with a certain amount of ability and plenty of dedication, with the right training and coaching he could help that boxer to become a champion.

CHAPTER 5

Fit to Box

Of all sports, the physical and mental demands of boxing must rate above any other. The boxer requires power in his legs, flexible hips and waist, a solid mid-section with a strong upper body. He also has to develop his lungs to help intensify his breathing and strengthen his heart, while building up stamina and physical endurance.

An amateur bout can only last for a maximum of either six or eight minutes, but it will be contested at such a pace that the whole body is worked at a very high intensity for two minutes of every round. No boxer can consider entering a boxing ring with intentions of competing unless he is in peak physical condition.

Some boxers may lack the natural ability of others but because of their dedication to training and way of life, they can succeed within the sport through their desire and determination. The boxer requires a conditioning programme specifically designed for him to become 'fit to box', with his routine being structured towards competition.

Cardiovascular Conditioning

Cardiovascular training strengthens the heart and lungs, increasing the body's ability to carry out strenuous tasks involving a large number of muscles over a long duration. Muscles must have a continuous supply of energy that is produced through oxygen intake.

Oxygen is the key to fitness, the more the body can process the fitter you will become. More energy can be produced when a greater volume of oxygen can be transported to the muscles by the blood. As the heart and lungs become more efficient the greater our endurance becomes.

An amateur boxing bout is basically anaerobic as short bursts of explosive energy are needed over a short duration. As aerobic training increases the amount of oxygen the body is able to process, it is just as important. For any activity to be classed as aerobic, duration needs to be a minimum of fifteen to twenty minutes.

There will, however, during high-intensive exercise come a point when everybody becomes tired and fatigued. At this point the body cannot take in sufficient oxygen to perform; this, of course, varies with each individual as the fitter you are the longer it will take to reach this point. When it is reached, the body will have to borrow oxygen from its reserves, which is known as oxygen debt. To continue with the physical activity you borrow more oxygen, causing a build-up of lactic acid in the bloodstream, stopping the body working and causing the muscles to cramp. Oxygen is taken from the atmosphere, being used by the body until a fresh supply of oxygen is needed.

Components of Fitness	
Frequency	How often training.
Intensity	Degree of strength, energy or difficulty during training.
Duration	How long spent training.
Overload	When the body is stimulated by the three components above, it will increase its capacity to perform, work and adopt to increasing physical demands.
Training Effect	Improvements in the physical changes in the body and fitness due to regular exercise, only occur if training is sufficient in all the three components (frequency, intensity and duration).

Aerobic	Training or exercise for which the lungs can supply sufficient oxygen.
Anaerobic	Training when insufficient oxygen is supplied.
Steady State	Oxygen supply meets demands.
Oxygen Debt	The amount of oxygen needed to return the body to normal after exercise.
Anaerobic Threshold	The point at which the body can no longer supply enough oxygen for the effort expended and goes into oxygen debt.
Stroke Volume	The volume of blood that is pumped out every time the heart contracts, multiplied by the heart rate.
Cardiac Output	The amount of blood pumped around the body by the heart in a minute.
VO_2 Max	Maximum oxygen intake that can be delivered to muscles during exercise.
Lactic Acid	By-product of anaerobic exercise. Muscles cannot contract while it is present.

Training Effects of Aerobic Exercise

- Strengthens heart and lungs
- Increases the amount of oxygen the body is able to process
- Burns fat, so increasing lean body tissue
- Speeds up metabolic rate
- Works large muscle groups.

The Heart Rate

To benefit from aerobic exercise the heart needs to be working between 60 per cent and 85 per cent of your maximum heart rate. To monitor pulse rate, heart monitors can be used or alternatively locating the anatomical site, carotid artery (neck) or radical artery (wrist) during or after exercise, check the pulse by placing forefingers on either site and count ten seconds times six.

Resting Heart Rate	Heart beat at rest before exercise.
Estimated Maximum Heart Rate	Rate at which your heart can beat for your age. 220 minus your age.
Estimated Target Rate	Working 60 per cent to 85 per cent of your maximum heart rate.
Recovery Heart Rate	When heart slows down after five minutes, heartbeat should equal less than 60 per cent of maximum.

Base Fitness

Due to the demanding physical requirements of boxing, it is beneficial for anyone entering his first training session to possess a certain amount of basic fitness. Before participating in anything as strenuous as boxing, it is always advisable to seek medical advice from your own doctor, even when possessing a good level of fitness.

Most amateur gyms will provide a basic training programme set out for its members. Normally this will consist of a warm-up, skipping, punch-bags, pad work, shadow boxing and sparring. Every station will be set at two-minute rounds followed by a one-minute rest, duplicating the duration of a bout. Groundwork completes the session along with static stretching.

A competitive boxer trains between four to six days per week, depending on the standard he is at. Besides his training in the gym, he will include running or roadwork in his routine. As training methods become more advanced, boxers are adding conditioning work such as weights and core training into their schedule, reaping the benefits of the extra power and strength gained from their inclusion. As with every sport, boxing training has moved with the times and many coaches adapt a more scientific approach towards their charges' training.

As in many other sports these new methods have to combine with the more traditional training techniques, but unlike most other sports it is difficult to prove whether a modern-day boxer is any fitter or stronger than boxers of the past.

Athletes are running faster, throwing further, jumping higher and longer and lifting heavier weights, but are boxers better conditioned today than they were centuries ago?

Over 300 years ago boxers battled bare knuckle for sometimes more than sixty rounds, competing till only one man was left standing. In 1790 Ben Brain and Bill Hooper fought for 187 rounds, lasting for three and a half hours. The bout finally ended in a draw as it became too dark for the fighters to see each other.

It is hard to imagine the physical strength and endurance that these men must have possessed and the pain they would have endured to fight for such a length of time. Training for an event such as this would surely have been very basic, as would the diet of the two fighters, yet these two men could give out and receive an amazing amount of punishment.

Obviously boxing today is far more technical and competed at a faster pace than was the case 300 years ago and, due to modern diet, boxers are bigger than they were then. James Corbett, the first heavyweight champion of the world, would only be a light-heavyweight if he were around today. Boxing has evolved over the years and technology provides an important role in the boxer's preparation.

Some coaches may prefer to stay with the more traditional forms of training while others feel that modern methods are the only way forward. Every boxer is different, so combining older forms of training with new ones will serve as a good combination to obtain the required results. Boxers and trainers should always keep an open mind as to both new and older ideas and never be afraid to experiment with training, especially during the close season.

Developing a Training Routine

It is said 'that hard training makes for an easy contest', although easy contests are a luxury that most boxers rarely experience. Putting in the work at the gym and reaching the best physical condition possible can be the difference between winning and losing.

Every seasoned boxer will have his own preferences in his training regime, depending on his style, strengths and weaknesses. His programme should be structured and balanced with a strong leaning towards competition, developing power, speed and endurance.

Boxing is a skill sport and training has to be focused on honing core techniques such as co-ordination, balance and timing.

A senior boxer is allowed to compete in a maximum of eighteen contests per season excluding championships and international matches, so a top experienced amateur has to be constantly prepared and always ready to compete. Once he has reached his peak during the course of a season, the boxer will need to be always ticking over to keep close to his peak condition. English championships are contested over a couple of months from area zone finals to the national finals. A boxer who reaches those finals has had to stay in top condition and maintain his weight throughout the whole of this period. Once a boxer has reached a certain level of competitive fitness, his sole aim is to stay at that level. There is always the danger of over-training, resulting in tiredness and sometimes injuries.

Finding a routine that will keep him in the shape and condition required, whilst having a nutrition plan to help him stay around his contest weight in between bouts, is the key. Even a boxer who has not entered into the championships and does not compete at international level but is a busy popular boxer can compete an average of twice a month during the season. Making weight for club shows is a little more relaxed, but he will always need to keep himself ready and prepared.

Once he has a training routine planned for his season, the boxer must try to keep to it as rigidly as possible. If everything is not going to plan and results are going against him, changes may need to be made. Boxers like any other athlete can become stale and sometimes need a fresh approach, although the middle of the season with bouts scheduled is not the time to bring in new, radical ideas. If changes are to be made they will usually be tactical and if fitness is a problem then there is something wrong with the boxer's training routine, or his health or mental approach.

Gary takes a small group of boxers running along a canal path, away from hard surfaces and exhaust fumes.

It is almost impossible to be at your peak for seven to eight months of the year as well as staying injury-free and healthy. A programme combining specific boxing skill training with strength and fitness work with a good diet and quality rest, will prepare a busy boxer for his season.

Running

To attain cardiovascular conditioning and aerobic fitness, it would be difficult to find another form of exercise more beneficial than running. For the boxer it is an essential part of his training routine to improve his endurance and stamina. During the off season, running distances between five to six miles at a steady pace two to three times per week is needed to maintain fitness and help reduce weight for the up and coming season. Towards competition time most amateur boxers taper off the distance of their running to between two to three miles, whilst increasing their pace. Professional boxers, due to the difference in style of boxing compared to the amateur and the longer duration of rounds and bouts, will tend to keep longer runs in their pre-contest preparation.

Amateur boxing is more of a sprint and because of the faster more explosive movements required, the amateur will often introduce more speed work into his weekly running routine during the competitive phase of his training. This is not to say that the professional does not include sprint work as part of his training, but he will often go more for distance on the road than the amateur.

Due to the constant pounding on the road when running, the coach will have to monitor closely his boxer's progress, as too much running on a hard surface can cause damage to ligaments and tendons. Heavyweights and super-heavyweights have to pay particular attention to their mileage, as anyone 90kg (198lb) plus is not really built for running long distances. The force of their weight pounding down on concrete paths or roads can cause too much damaging force on knees and shins due to the impact. This is why many coaches take the approach of quality not quantity and a series of high intensive sprints on a track or grass will not only be more specifically aimed towards a boxer's conditioning, but will replace the long miles of pounding the joints.

When running on a regular basis it is vitally important to wear correctly fitting training shoes, designed especially for running. The days of boxers running in heavy boots to add power to the legs are well gone – if possible, find a sports outlet that specializes in running shoes.

Speed Work

Speed work can be incorporated into training sessions through interval running or fartleck, which is a Swedish term for speed play. This form of running will not only work the anaerobic system but will also aid the boxer's recovery between repeated efforts. By varying the distance, duration, speed and intensity of each repetition, the training load on the body will be increased. Interval training performed at maximum effort will develop speed, power and strength.

Speed work can be performed almost any-where, but it would be a major advantage if access to a running track were available.

Below is an example of interval drills for an intermediate to advanced athlete. Novices should halve the distance and all athletes must warm up with a steady jog of about ten minutes.

Rest 10 minutes between sets and 5-minutes between repetitions:

2 × 400 metres
3 × 200 metres
3 × 100 metres

Warm down with a 5-minute jog and stretch.

Repetitions and sets can vary by alternating distances. Keep a record of split times and try to improve on speed each session.

If a running track is not available, similar drills can be carried out at a park or road using markers such as lampposts or trees. Most boxing gyms will not possess such equipment as running machines, so if the boxer is a member of a health club or leisure centre, speed play can be performed on the treadmill. These are ideal for accurate distance and pace monitoring and have the advantage of being sited indoors, which can be an asset during the winter months.

Hill Reps

Once proficient in speed play on the flat surface, incline sprints are the next phase of the interval-training programme. Drills can be performed over distance or time, for example 5 × 100 metres or 5 × 1-minute reps, or 3 × 200 metres or 3 × 2-minute

The boxing gym. A good gym must have a selection of punch-bags and a ring.

reps. Hills must be run at full effort, then descent should be used for a slow recovery period, this combination being then repeated. Always remember to warm up and cool down with a 5- to 10-minute gentle jog.

The Boxing Gym

The gym is the place where the core of the boxer's training routine is carried out. Even the most basic of gyms will need to be equipped with a selection of bags to punch, mirrors to assess technique, space to skip and a ring to put all that skill, technique and fitness to the test.

The Warm-Up

Before every training session a warm-up period of about ten minutes is required. Light mobility work performed at a moderate pace will help prepare the body for vigorous exercise. The warm-up slowly increases the heart rate whilst also raising muscle temperature and increasing flexibility of the joints and circulation to the tissues surrounding the joints. The whole of the body from head to toe will need to be warmed up, starting with small movements including shoulder rolls and neck stretches and building up to larger moves to include arm swings and knee lifts. Once core temperature of the body is raised, training can begin.

Punch-Bags

Good bags are vital to the gym for the coach to teach his students the correct and safe way to deliver a punch. There is a wide variety of bags, all of which help the boxer improve his style while adding power and snap to his punches. The basic bag is long, straight and made of either leather or a tough PVC that comes in different weights and sizes.

A heavy bag is a large, solid bag designed to help increase power to the individual's punch. A good heavy bag will have very little movement, which enables the boxer to practise working at close quarters, improving his in-fighting techniques. If a boxer has a tendency to rely on heavy punches while neglecting his boxing ability and point-scoring punches, he should be advised to spend a little more time on the lighter bags. As these bags have more movement, it will encourage more attention to footwork, moving in and out from the bag and punching from angles. Both bags are excellent for improving punching technique and the boxer has to work on them with equal regularity.

Other bags like the angle bag and the heavy maize ball are also important when trying combination punches and are ideal for use in perfecting hooks and uppercuts. Nearly every boxing club will have in its gym a floor-to-ceiling ball. This is a favourite with a lot of coaches, as its movement and unpredictability is likened to a live opponent. The floor-to-ceiling and the small maize ball are skill bags, so fast hands and quick footwork are needed when using them. Eye-to-hand co-ordination will be greatly improved.

The maize bag.

The floor to ceiling ball.

The heavy bag.

Shadow Boxing

This helps the boxer focus on competition strategy, working on attacks and defensive moves against an imaginary opponent. If the ring is available, it is an ideal opportunity to practise skill and ring craft. Techniques such as drawing and feinting an opponent or working off the ropes can be mastered during shadow boxing sessions. Using a full-length mirror is also useful for checking stance and guard.

Skipping

Skipping improves rhythm, balance and helps co-ordination of the feet. Arms are kept tight to the side of the body with only the wrists turning. Footwork should be light whilst moving in various directions.

Skipping.

Training Tip

During training, treat every exercise as if you are in an actual contest. When moving away from the bag keep the arms up in their defensive position, as if moving away from an opponent. Never switch off for a second and acquire bad habits, just because the bag cannot hit you back. The same applies during shadow boxing and even when skipping, as short fast spurts can be added, following the same pattern as a bout.

Circuit Training

This is one of the major components of the boxer's conditioning programmes and needs to be featured in every boxing club. It is as important to a boxer in assisting him to reach the degree of fitness he requires, as is his running or gym work.

Due to the space needed to accommodate a circuit training routine, staggered individual training times and pure numbers of boxers in the gym, circuits are sometimes not that practical. A coach must find ways of incorporating this important aspect of the boxer's fitness training into his regular routine. The easiest form of circuits to organize is the fixed load circuits, like the 'ton up' that can be carried out individually or in a group format. No equipment is required so space should not present a problem. The 'ton up' consists of ten exercises timed by ten repetitions, 'the ton'. Each exercise follows continually without rest.

Exercises used in such circuits need to be dynamic with emphasis on speed and power. Although performed as quickly as possible, good form has to be maintained at all times on each exercise. No one major muscle group should be worked back to back, so it is important to try and alternate per body part. Record the time taken during each 'ton up' and try to improve on each attempt.

Example 'Ton up'

10 × 10 repetitions

Exercise

(1) Tuck Jumps

- Stand with feet together and hands by the side
- Jump high bringing knees to chest
- Land softly.

(2) Press-ups

- Feet on the ground, hands greater than shoulder-width apart
- Arms fully extended with palms of the hands on floor
- Bend elbows till chest is just above floor level
- Push upwards till arms are fully extended.

The press-up. Start with arms outstretched...

...bring chest down to a few inches off the floor.

(3) Burpee Jumps

- Start in press-up position
- Bring knees towards chest
- Jump high with arms and legs straight
- Land softly into crouch position and extend legs to start position.

The burpee jump. From the press-up position, bring knees towards the arms...

...then jump into the air with arms at the side.

(4) Tummy Crunches

- Lie on back with hands on side of head and legs elevated
- Sit up, bringing knees to elbows
- Lower and repeat.

Tummy crunch. Lie on back with legs elevated, sit up bringing elbows towards the knees.

Alternate thrust. From press-up position, alternate knees to elbows.

(5) Split Jumps

- Start in squat position with hands on floor
- Jump up, twisting body and changing leading leg whilst in the air
- Land in a deep squat, with soft knees.

(6) Dorsal Raise

- Lie on front, legs outstretched and hands in small of back
- Raise head and chest with control, then lower.

(8) Snake Press

- Start with feet and hands shoulder-width apart
- Back side is high in the air forming an inverted 'v' position
- Push with the legs and bending the elbows scoop chest towards the floor, then extend arms fully.

The snake press. Push with legs, whilst scooping chest and head towards floor.

Dorsal raise. Lift head and chest off the floor whilst keeping arms in the small of the back and feet on the ground.

(7) Alternate Thrust

- Start in press-up position
- Alternately bring knees to elbows.

Finish move with arms fully extended.

(9) V Sit-Up

- Lie flat on the floor with legs and arms outstretched
- Thrust arms and legs into the air until fingers touch the toes, creating a 'v' shape.

(10) Star Jumps

- Start from a deep squat position
- Spring as high as possible with arms and legs out into a star position
- Land softly into a deep squat.

The V sit-up. Lie outstretched on the floor.

Bring body upwards into a V position.

Timed circuits or target circuits are set against the clock, aiming at attempting as many repetitions as possible per exercise within the set time.

Equipment can be added to various stations, such as free weights or medicine balls to add resistance to the effort. Using a step or bench over 12 inches in height or if the gym possesses a raised ring, step-ups, box jumps or dips are just three exercises that can be added to the circuit. If space allows, apparatus can be included for sprint work and footwork drills. Cones can be used as markers for shuttle runs or an agility ladder for footwork drills.

Ten exercises timed at thirty seconds per station moving continuously will push the boxers for five minutes of non-stop highly intensive efforts. After a short recovery period, circuits can be repeated. If space and equipment is not available stations can be designed for body resistance exercises, as in the ton up.

In busy clubs, stations can be set for each participant to work with a partner. This example circuit is set for a gym with sufficient space and apparatus; coaches can design their circuits accordingly towards their club and boxers' needs.

- Stations should alternate major muscle groups
- Exercises for circuits should be emphasized on speed and power
- As many repetitions as possible should be attempted within given time
- Good form must be kept throughout each exercise
- Keep a record of repetitions performed on each station and try to improve with every circuit.

(1) Shuttle Runs

- Can be run over a variety of distances with various markers
- Sprint from start to first marker and back to start
- Keep repeating with each marker.

(2) Alternate Shoulder Press

- Place a barbell on the back of the shoulders
- Outstretch arms upwards and bring barbell down to front shoulders
- Alternate between front and back.

(3) Alternate Step-ups (with dumbbells)

- Hold a dumbbell in each hand
- With leading leg step onto the step with the whole foot on top
- Bring up other foot as leading foot steps down
- Then change leading leg.

(4) Bench Dips

- Hands shoulder-width apart, palms down on bench, legs outstretched
- Bend elbows until bottom almost touches floor, then extend arms.

(5) Sit-up and Punch (with hand-weights)

- Lie on back with feet shoulder-width apart on floor or on a bench
- Sit-up and punch with both hands whilst holding hand-weights.

(6) Squats (with medicine ball)

- Feet shoulder-width apart, hold medicine ball
- Squat down, keeping back straight and head up with thighs parallel to the floor, then jump up when returning to start position.

(7) Alternate Dumbbell Press

- Stand with feet shoulder-width apart and knees slightly bent
- Hold a dumbbell in each hand at shoulder level with elbows bent
- Extend each arm until fully outstretched.

(8) Bench Strides

- Stand with feet together on bench
- Jump down, with soft knees and each foot either side of the bench
- Spring back up onto bench and repeat.

(9) Sit-ups (with medicine ball)

- Lie on floor, feet shoulder-width apart with medicine ball held into chest
- Sit up holding medicine ball and repeat.

(10) Dumbbell Shrugs

- Stand with feet shoulder-width apart
- Hold a dumbbell in each hand with arms down at the side of the body
- Shrug shoulders towards ear lobes keeping arms extended.

CHAPTER 6

Groundwork

Groundwork is the fine-tuning of the boxer's conditioning work. If he really wants to succeed and take his training routine onto another level, he must be prepared to put in the extra work to improve his strength, power, speed and flexibility. The modern-day coach needs to familiarize himself with other forms of training, besides the traditional boxing format.

Coaches should be able to advise their boxers on what additional types of training they need to help them become the complete athlete. If a boxer lacks physical strength he may be advised to go on a weight-training programme, or if he has a weak lower back or tummy muscles, then core stability would be advisable. A boxer may still find he has problems generating the explosive power he needs to sustain attacks on his opponent, but introducing plyometrics (explosive movements) into his regular training routine may solve this flaw.

Certain coaches might be of the opinion that all training has to be boxing-based and feel that using resistance exercises like weight-training could cause muscle strains and also slow the boxer down by bulking him up too much. Other coaches may feel that they are not qualified enough in other forms of training to offer constructive advice.

Many top professional boxer's employ the services of a strength-conditioning coach, but to the unpaid amateur this is a luxury that many may not be able to afford. Many boxing clubs will not have the facilities available to carry out a serious weight-training routine, so these sessions may need to be carried out at a gym specializing in weight training. Core work and plyometrics could be performed within a boxing gym.

Professional boxing due to its longer duration is aerobic and anaerobic; amateur boxing is likened to a sprint. Although, as already documented, aerobic fitness is needed in preparation for a contest, an actual amateur bout is purely anaerobic. Due to its anaerobic requirements, the conditioning phase of the amateur boxer's training can be similar to that of the sprinter.

'Explosive' is a word constantly used in this book but the amateur contest, like the 100 metre and 200 metre sprint, is just that, explosive. Explosive movements increase through strength, power and speed and below are various ways of achieving all three.

Weight Training

Progressive resistance exercise is a very important aspect of modern sport preparation, especially for the athlete whose sport requires dynamic power. Weight-training for boxing should never be confused with body-building, as the boxer's main aim is to build his strength for his sport. His basic objective is to develop power in the form of strength and speed-training. Due to a lack of basic strength, skill can be affected as can mobility, so a structured weight-training programme designed to strengthen muscles and ligaments will not only increase the overall power of the boxer, but will also minimize the risk of joint injuries whilst aiding in a quick recovery.

There is a misconception that weight-training for the sports person requires a programme of light weights and high repetitions. To develop strength and power, training should consist of heavier weights and lower reps. Speed is dependent on increases in strength and power and the boxer needs a greater supply required than his sports limits demands.

The weight programme most suited to the boxer's requirements would be based around compound exercises. This is when exercises involved are of a massive nature, using large muscle groups per set. Opposite to this would be isolation exercises that concentrate on working each muscle at a time, aiming more towards shaping and improving definition. Compound-style workouts are best suited to free weights as opposed to selecterized machines, due to the power drive required for weight-lifting. It is always advisable to work with a trainer or training partner when working on a strength routine that involves heavy poundage. To achieve power from weight-training, repetitions per set should be to pre-exhaust, which is attempting a poundage just below your one repetition maximum (1RM).

For example, working three sets per exercise, the first set's poundage would be at 60–70 per cent of your 1RM, looking to complete 5–6 reps. The second set at 75–85 per cent for 3–5 reps, with the third and final set at 85–90 per cent for 1–4 reps. As the work carried out for such a routine is at almost maximum weight, it should never be attempted without the aid of somebody spotting for you, especially such exercises as squats, bench press or shoulder press.

Basic Strength Programme

Squat

- From standing position place bar on shoulders
- Overhand wide grip

The squat. Start from a standing position.

On the squat do not bring hips below the knees.

- Feet shoulder-width apart with toes slightly outwards
- Keep heels on floor at all times
- Look straight ahead or slightly upwards
- At deepest point of squat, hips and thighs are parallel with knees.

Breathing

- Inhale on downward motion, exhale on upward motion.

Major Muscles Working

- Thighs (quadriceps)
- Bottom (gluteus maximus)
- Lower back (erector spinae).

Bench Press

- Lie flat on bench with feet firmly on the ground
- Wide overhand grip on bar
- Lift and slowly lower to the chest
- On press, lock out arms fully.

Breathing

- Inhale on downward motion, exhale on upward motion.

Major Muscles Working

- Chest (pectoral)
- Shoulders (deltoids)
- Rear of arms (triceps).

Bench press. Bring bar down to the chest and fully lock arms out on press.

The dead lift. Start from a deep squat position, with alternate hand grip to help obtain a better lift.

Dead Lift

- Hands shoulder-width apart with alternate grip, between over and under
- Back kept arched, never rounded throughout movement
- Lift bar with knees bent and arms locked out
- On lift drive hips forward, straightening legs with a slight extension of back.

Breathing

- Inhale on upward motion, exhale on downward motion.

Major Muscles Working

- Quadriceps
- Hamstrings
- Gluteus maximus
- Erector spinae.

Bent-Over Rows

- Bend forward with straight back and knees slightly bent and arms locked out
- Wide overhand grip on bar pulling bar towards chest
- Once bar reaches chest, lower towards floor.

Breathing

- Inhale on upward motion, exhale on downward motion.

On upward motion slightly extend the back.

Major Muscles Working

- Upper Back (latissimus dorsi).

Behind Neck Press

- Can be done in a standing or sitting position. When standing, keep feet shoulder-width apart with knees slightly bent. When seated keep back firmly pressed into back rest, with both feet on the ground

The shrugs. Bring shoulders up towards the ears.

Breathing

- Inhale on upward motion, exhale on downward motion.

Major Muscles Working

- Neck (trapezius)
- Deltoids.

No specific arm exercises are needed as the triceps, which make up most of the arm and are instrumental in the punching technique, will be used during the bench and shoulder press. No exercises are required for the front of the arm (bicep) as this tends to shorten the arm, which would be detrimental to the boxer. If arms are particularly weak, bench or parallel bar dips can be done.

- During heavy lifting a weight-training belt will help support the lower back
- Always use collars on bars and dumbbells.

Muscle Contraction

There are approximately 650 muscles in the human body and almost every muscle will be brought into play during a boxing bout. Single muscle fibres are composed of a number of myofibrils that are elastic rod-like subfibres that lie lengthways in the cell. They are the basic contractions within the fibre and as the myofibrils contract this causes the fibres

Press behind the neck, fully lock out arms on the press.

- Rest bar on shoulders with overhand grip, just over shoulder-width apart
- Push bar above head until arms fully lock out.

Breathing

- Inhale on upward motion, exhale on downward motion.

Major Muscles Working

- Deltoids
- Triceps.

Shrugs

- Grip bar with hands shoulder-width apart and an overhand grip
- Keep arms straight and raise shoulders towards ear lobes.

to contract, which, in turn, will cause the muscle to contract. The nerve cells (neurons) originate from the brain and control the pattern of muscle contractions. Neurons transfer messages to the motor neuron by stretching down the spinal cord and applying control of the muscles. The motor neuron and muscle fibres that it controls are known as the motor unit, which consists of hundreds of muscle fibres. Within the motor unit the nerve fibres and muscle fibres may or may not respond to a stimulus.

The strength of the contractions of an individual motor unit is controlled by the total number of times each motor unit is stimulated per second. Energy for muscular contraction is required for all types of physical activity. An immediate surge of energy in the muscles comes from adenosine triphosphate (ATP), an energy-rich compound, that is only stored in trace amounts in the muscle cells. The body has to produce ATP for muscular contraction, as without it the muscle will not respond. This can be produced by having a good supply of oxygen to the muscles, through aerobic and anaerobic training and fuelling the body with carbohydrates in the form of glycogen and fats in the form of free fatty acids.

Components of Strengths

1. Isometric – force is developed against an immovable object.
2. Isotonic – force is applied against a constant movable resistance.
   a) Concentric – when muscles shorten
   b) Eccentric – returns to normal range
3. Isokinetic – force is developed against a variable resistance of constant velocity.

Muscle Balancing

- Agonist – The primary muscle worked.
- Antagonist – The opposing muscle.

For every primary muscle worked (agonist) the opposing muscle (antagonist) must also be worked. Working opposing muscle groups lessens the possibility of muscular imbalance and reduces injury.

Fast- and Slow-Twitch Muscle Fibres

In any sport or training routine carried out by the athlete, one of the two muscle fibres are used. For any physical effort lasting longer than ten seconds the Red – Slow-Twitch Muscle Fibres (Type I) are called upon. Distance running, swimming and cycling are the type of endurance sports that are certainly using mostly red muscle fibres. In shorter sporting activities, of a more explosive nature, such as athletic field events, 100 metres sprint and weight-lifting, White – Fast-Twitch Muscle Fibres (Type II) would predominately be used.

In some sports, for example boxing, both muscle fibres are used. A round in an amateur boxing bout lasts for two minutes, which is obviously more than the ten seconds time factor needed to decide which type of fibres are used. A boxing bout will have fast, short, bursts of intense activity, immediately followed by periods in which both boxers are searching for openings to out manoeuvre his opponent. This means that the boxer would be mostly using white – fast-twitch muscle fibres. The following routine will help develop the force and energy needed to maximize explosive power from the fast-twitch muscle fibres.

Plyometrics

First used by Eastern European track and field athletes in the 1960s, plyometrics has played a major role in athletic improvements over the last few decades. It is a form of exercise that involves explosive movements increasing speed, strength and power, whilst aiding agility. They are dynamic routines that are specifically directed towards the athlete's sport. The boxer requires explosive leg action, strong hips, waist and upper body. To improve efficiency, drills are performed at maximum force, ensuring improvements of starting and explosive strength. Drills for plyometrics are a sequence of jumping, bouncing, hopping and bounding movements, performed at a high velocity. Strict form has to be maintained throughout each repetition, paying particular attention to safety. When making impact with the floor after landing from high jumping-type movements, employ special care towards knees and ankle protection.

Example Routine:

Vertical Jump	Stand with feet together and arms at the side. Spring high into the air bringing both arms outstretched overhead. Land with both feet on the ground with soft knees.
Press-ups and Clap	Performed as the basic press-up, clapping hands on the push-up.
Box Jumps	Use a box or a step that measure more than 12in. From a standing position, jump onto the box/step with both feet fully landing on the top and both knees soft.
Medicine Ball Sit-Ups	If training with a partner, sit up and throw the ball to partner, maintaining the sit-up position until partner throws the ball back, then repeat the sequence. If training alone, lie back with arms outstretched, holding ball, sit up and bring ball to front.
Pike Jumps	From standing position jump as high as possible, outstretching legs and arms forwards, with fingertips reaching towards toes.
Stomach Bounce off Medicine Ball	Place medicine ball on the floor, supporting body with the arms. Vigorously bounce the front and sides of the mid-section of the abdominals on the ball.
Alternate Leg Bound or Hops	Depending on space, bound or hop from one marker to another. If space is limited, replace this exercise with tuck or star jumps.
Medicine Ball Twist	Stand with feet shoulder-width apart with knees slightly bent. Clutch medicine ball tightly into chest and twist from side to side. Keep legs still, maintaining a solid base.

Plyometric exercise is made up of explosive movements using jumping and bounding exercises, such as star jumps...

...tuck jumps...

...and split jumps. Starting from a squat position...

... jump with an explosive thrust from the legs, whilst turning in mid-air and landing back into a deep squat.

Horizontal jumps with arms to the side, as shown, or a vertical jump with arms outstretched above the head. Both excellent plyometric exercises.

Box jump. The higher the box the more explosive strength in the legs required.

Pike jump.

The sample routine above combines high bursts of power within the leg section with ballistic upper and lower body strength work.

Warm up for 10–15min with light mobility work. When first attempting plyometric drills, begin with 1–2 sets of six repetitions per exercise, building towards three sets of 8–10 repetitions. Rest for one minute between sets.

To increase the intensity from this routine, a power circuit can de devised. This can be done by incorporating exercises from the weight programme and working them back-to-back with exercises from the plyometric programme. For example, perform a set of squats where 10–12 repetitions can be completed before pre-exhaustion; this is immediately followed by 10–12 repetitions of tuck jumps. After the two sets are completed rest for two minutes, then proceed with the next two sets working the upper body

Medicine ball sit-up with partner.

Sit-ups performed on a Swiss ball.

– for example, bench press followed by press-up and clap. Do ten exercises per circuit, rest five minutes between each circuit and try to complete three full circuits.

Speed and Agility Training

New forms of training can be added into the boxer's routine by introducing equipment such as agility ladders, step hurdles and marker cones. These types of circuits have been part of the footballer's and rugby player's training for some time. They can be used outdoors or indoors and help promote fast feet, agility and co-ordination. Resistance can be added by wearing a weighted training vest. This type of training is not only a high-intensity work-out, but will assist with the boxer's footwork.

Core Stability

Core work has become a very important aspect of every athlete's training routine. The core of the body is the lower back, deep abdominal and oblique muscles that are found in the waist. Most core exercises are performed on a large inflated ball, known as a Swiss ball. These balls have been used by sports physiotherapists for rehabilitation work with athletes for over thirty years.

When performing exercises on the ball the athlete's feet need to be firmly planted on the floor

hip-width apart to ensure stability of the ball; this helps isolate the muscles that are being worked. Exercises such as weight-training, abdominal work along with stretching exercises can all be performed on one of these balls.

In addition to the ball, core boards are now available that work on the same principle, allowing the athlete to exercise whilst standing on the board activating core stability. Building a strong core is vital to the boxer, as he requires a strong mid-section to allow him to twist and pivot with force.

Stretching

It has always been accepted that stretching pre- and post-workout is a vital part of any athlete's training session. For many years, fitness instructors and coaches have emphasized the important role that stretching plays in the prevention of muscle soreness and injuries. Mobility warm-ups designed to raise the body's core temperature, whilst also increasing the flow of blood to the muscles, have always been preceded by a short duration of static stretches. Studies have found that stretching immediately after a warm-up can cause minor tears in the muscles, leading many fitness experts and physiotherapists to believe that stretching provides no protection against muscle injury whatsoever. If this is the case and as stretching is usually the most disliked and ignored section of any boxer's training, why bother?

Stretching can improve strength and posture, but above all the most beneficial component of improvement for the boxer is the increased flexibility that stretching provides. Improved flexibility provides a better range of motion available in a single or group of joints, enabling the boxer to possess more freedom of movement. There are various forms of stretching with static stretching being the most commonly used post-work-out. This is carried out by extending the muscle in question to a point of tension for 15–20 seconds just prior to the lengthening of the muscle causing pain or discomfort.

Once vigorous training is completed, 10-minute static stretching will not only assist in loosening tight muscles that have been used during the session, but it will also aid recovery by allowing the athlete to reduce the heart rate, whilst breathing returns to normal. We have already covered the importance of breathing in an earlier chapter, but correct breathing techniques during training have to be maintained. During high-intensity training, breathing too hard may cause light-headedness, whilst holding the breath can cause what is known as Valsalva manoeuvre, which is the closing of the glottis, creating pressure in the chest cavity leading to a rise in blood pressure. Breathing should follow a consistent rhythmic pattern and a 10-minute cool down, as it is known, will allow the body time to follow a steady breathing pattern.

To stop vigorous exercise abruptly can cause the blood to pool in the arms and legs. Once you have finished training never drop the head lower than the heart, as a sudden rush of blood to the head may result in dizziness. Stretching as much as anything provides the boxer with a relaxation period after an intensive training session, allowing him to fully recover. Other forms of stretching include dynamic stretching, which can be likened to the ones in the mobility warm-up section. Theses exercises are to be performed moderately and smoothly, gently stretching to the end part of the motion.

Stretching where a partner or trainer can be used is termed proprioceptive neuromuscular facilitation (PNF). This involves the boxer contracting the muscle as his partner/trainer applies light pressure with the boxer resisting the force. This allows the stretch to reach its full range of motion. The stretch is held for ten seconds, relaxed and extended slightly further and held for another ten seconds. It is important to be aware of your limitations during the stretch, informing your partner/trainer when the full range has been reached. Ballistic stretches are best avoided as the jerky, bouncy movements can put unnecessary stress on the joints. To aid the body's prevention mechanism during stretching it is armed with sensory receptors called Golgi tendon organs, which are located at the muscular tendon junctures. Once a stretch has been commanded it will initiate a stimulation from the GTOs into an inhibitory or relaxation response, ten seconds being the minimum amount of time necessary to effect GTOs. The body also has a protective mechanism against severe injury, known as stretch reflex. This comes into action once a muscle is stretched too quickly.

Flexibility

Possessing good flexibility is a major advantage to the boxer as he will always require a good range of movement. The boxer needs to move forward, backwards and laterally, while also having good trunk rotation. Flexibility will also enhance his evasive ability, enabling him to slip, roll and duck from attacking punches.

Everyone functions within three planes of motion that divide the joint action of the body.

Sagittal Plane	Forward and backward motions.
Frontal Plane	Side-to-side motion.
Transverse Plane	Rotational motion. Complete turn movement around fixed joint.
Joint Action:	
Flexion	The quality of large movement of a joint.
Extension	The opening of the joint. The opposite to flexion.
Abduction	Is to take away from the mid-line of the body.
Adduction	Is to bring in.

COOL-DOWN STRETCHES

Tricep Stretch

Place right hand on the back of the left shoulder with the left hand cupped around right elbow. Hold for ten seconds and repeat with other arm.

Back Stretch

Curve spine and outstretch with both arms to the front with hands clasped together.

Chest Stretch

Hold arms outstretched behind the back with hands clasped together.

Shoulder Stretch

Stretch arms downwards, clasping hands together.

Quad Stretch

Stand on left leg while pulling right foot behind yourself. Outstretch left arm for balance. Hold and repeat on opposite leg.

Lunge Stretch

Bend right leg while outstretching left leg in lunge position. Place hands on right thigh for support. Hold and repeat on opposite leg.

Chest stretch.   Shoulder stretch.

Tricep stretch.   Back stretch.   Quad stretch.   Lunge stretch.

Calf Stretch

Straightening right leg, place right heel onto floor with toes facing upwards. Bend left leg, while placing both hands on left thigh. Hold and repeat on opposite leg.

Lying Leg Stretch

Lie on back with left leg bent and foot flat on floor. Bring right leg upwards, holding at ankle and calf, bring head towards knee. Hold and repeat on opposite leg.

Lower Back and Glute Stretch

Seated on floor with both legs outstretched, bring right leg over left leg, whilst looking over right shoulder. Hold and repeat on opposite side.

Cat Stretch

Kneel down on all fours whilst placing forehead to the ground with arms outstretched.

Stretching Tips

On all standing stretches have soft knee, tummy tucked in and shoulders back.

Hold each stretch for 10–20sec.

Never overstretch, only stretch to a point of minor tension within the muscles.

Keep stretches static without bouncing through the stretch.

Always maintain good form.

Calf stretch.

Lower back and glute stretch.

Lying leg stretch.

Cat stretch.

There are other ways of helping the muscles recover from strenuous exercises and trying to prevent strains and injuries. One that has been used by sports people for some time is taking an ice bath. For many years most athletes found soaking in a hot tub the most efficient way to soothe aching muscles, but this can cause micro tears in the muscles to bleed out, causing more pain. Sitting in a tub of iced cold water for approximately five minutes after a hard running training session, will flush out the lactic acid from the muscles, relieving the soreness and building the immune system.

Sports massage is another form of helping rid the body of aches and pains. A good massage can also bring relief to any recurring injuries that the boxer might be experiencing through his work-outs. It is important that when taking a massage, it is carried out by a fully qualified masseur.

Supplements can boost the boxer's diet but they can also keep the joints lubricated and supple. Cod liver or glucosamine sulphate are generally found to be the best forms of supplement to help promote healthy joints. Glucosamine is especially effective as it is involved in the maintenance of our connective tissue, such as cartilage, tendons and ligaments. The role of the connective tissue is to hold the bones together.

Anatomical Terms

The boxer needs to know his own body and a little knowledge in kinesiology and anatomy can be very useful towards injury prevention. The box lists six parts of the anatomy that could be injured by being overstressed through intensive training.

Active Rest

Some athletes, especially boxers, find great difficulty in doing no exercise whatsoever on their rest days. For someone who struggles to relax totally, active rest can be a useful way of performing light

Bone	Hard body structure that makes up the human skeleton.
Muscle	Organ that moves body parts.
Joint	Contact between two or more bones.
Ligament	Attaches bone to bone, generally elastic.
Tendon	Attaches muscle to bone.
Cartilage	Elastic tissue that is mostly converted into bone.

exercises that can be fun whilst not placing the body under unnecessary stress. Active rest can range from swimmimg a few steady lengths at the local pool, to going on a gentle bike ride or going for a leisurely walk.

It can never be overemphasized how important rest is and at least one day a week should be dedicated to complete relaxation. Cross-training techniques such as swimming and cycling can be a useful addition to the boxer's training programme, especially if he is carrying injuries that could be aggravated by running. Sprint intervals in the pool or on the bike can be just as demanding as running, but are non-impact. Alternating your training like this will not only minimize stress on the body but will help combat boredom and staleness that can be acquired when carrying out the same routines on a daily basis.

CHAPTER 7
Making the Weight

THE WEIGH-IN

Ask any boxer which aspect of the sport he dislikes the most and a high percentage will often claim 'making the weight'. Outside the super-heavyweight division the boxer will nearly always be attempting to lose weight, especially in the championships when trying to come in at the maximum of his weight category. It can be a big disadvantage weighing less than your opponent. This can act as a major factor in the performance, not only physically but also psychologically.

Making the weight in the championships is vital, as to misjudge the weight and 'come in' too heavy can result in all the hard work in the gym being in vain. Competitors are permitted a certain amount of time to shed the excess weight by skipping, shadow boxing, running or any other form of exercise that will assist in the boxer losing the additional kilos. To try and dry out on the day of the bout can be a dangerous practice; having to lose just one kilo can leave the boxer drained both physically and mentally.

If, for example, the boxer is struggling to make the middleweight limit of 75kg (165lb), his next category up will be at the light-heavyweight division at 81kg (178lb). If his natural weight is around 76kg (167lb) he could be competing against opponents of 6kg (13lb) heavier, which would mean giving away approximately one stone in weight. This would obviously leave the lighter boxer with a massive disadvantage and no coach would allow his charge to give so much weight away to his opponent.

It is for this reason that the boxer will almost certainly drop down to the maximum of his preferred weight category. Some boxers are always naturally at their weight level and may even favour competing a couple of kilos below the maximum. By coming in slightly lighter the boxer could feel that it might help with his speed and movement, but it must be taken into account that once training is stepped up to reach peak level, the weight will often automatically start to decrease. Making the weight can be seen as an art form and it begins in the morning at breakfast and goes right through to the training session in the gym. A good coach will always try to bring his boxer right inside the weight limit, so as not to give the opponent any physical advantage.

As previously covered in an earlier chapter, making the weight for club shows can be a little more relaxed, although the boxer will always want to compete at his strongest weight. Training and following a nutritional food plan to reach the

Super-heavyweights, such as these two boxers, do not need to make the weight, as they can box at any weight over 91kg (200lb).

desired weight is all part of the boxer's make-up and it usually helps to drive and keep him focused and motivated, whilst adding an extra edge to his training and character.

Traditionally professional boxers always weighed in on the morning of a bout, until in an attempt to make the sport safer a 24-hour weigh-in was introduced. The governing bodies and the medical authorities believed that the period between the weigh-in and the bout did not allow substantial time to re-hydrate the body. This, they felt, often left the boxer weak, which could lead to injuries or even fatalities. Twenty-four-hour weigh-ins were then introduced, purely as a safety measure, but this did not go ahead without its critics. In many World Championship bouts a boxer can weigh-in looking sinewy, ripped and sometimes drained. It is obvious from his appearance that he has had to really boil down the body to come in at the correct weight. On the very next day the same boxer walks into the ring with his muscles looking fuller and his whole body physically far larger.

He still looks in marvellous shape but it is plain to see that over the last twenty-four hours he has put on a remarkable amount of weight. It is not unusual for some boxers to enter the ring over 10 pounds heavier than they were the previous day. It is amazing that anyone could gain so much weight in such a short period of time, which could appear to give the naturally heavier boxer the advantage.

In the amateurs, the boxers weigh in a few hours prior to the contest, which does not allow much time to replenish the body, although most amateurs competing at 10 pounds over the weight they have strived to reach would leave them slow and lethargic. Major international events like the Olympics, Commonwealth Games and the World and European Championships really test the boxer's resistance, desire and above all his commitment to his sport. For a person to progress to the final stages of any of these tournaments they would have to compete in approximately five bouts within a period of between seven or fourteen days, depending on the event. For each one of these bouts the boxer would have had to come in within the limit of the weight category. For the boxers to compete in so many bouts in such a

short period of time would be extremely demanding, whilst also having to stay physically fit and strong, mentally focused, injury-free and restricting their daily food intake.

Usually after a hard contested bout a boxer will feel the need to refuel his body with some of the foods sacrificed, but until the boxer is out of the competition his weight is constantly monitored. Experienced boxers who have taken part in numerous championships and tournaments gain a good understanding of their own body. They will know what they can and can not eat, at what times and how their body will respond. Reaching the desired weight just at the right time whilst not leaving himself drained and weak is what makes a champion.

Many professional boxers employ the services of nutritionists and more top amateurs are also turning to qualified assistance. Most people know what they should and should not be eating, but the athlete, especially in the sport of boxing where weight plays such an important role, needs to have a greater knowledge of food than most. No one diet plan will be for everyone, as food requirements and taste vary from one person to another, so working with a professional nutrionist could be a very worthwhile investment.

When competing in any sport with weight categories, care must be taken when attempting to achieve the target. It could be dangerous for any athlete to lose too much weight in a short period of time and then compete in a strenuous sporting event. For anyone involved in combat sports, particularly boxing, the danger element increases. Losing weight too quickly has to be avoided, as the boxer should always try to be in training close to his contest weight. Ideally he needs to be training 2.3kg (5lb) within his weight and gradually come down to his weight category limit. It is definitely not advisable to compete in a weight division that is well under his natural weight. If he is constantly looking to lose 5kg (11lb) or more to make weight, he should be thinking about moving up to the next category.

The boxer must avoid reducing food and fluid intake by too much, as this can result in a decrease in body fluid and glycogen. This will leave the boxer with the difficult task of attempting to replenish his body in time for the contest. If he has dehydrated too much it can take days not hours to rehydrate and re-fuel the body. An advisable weight loss for the average lean boxer would be approximately 1kg (2lb) per week, with the boxer achieving his desired weight level at about three to four days before the bout. Losing weight at this rate should not affect the fluid or glycogen stored within the body. Starvation diets and dehydration to make the weight can cause low blood glucose levels resulting in low liver glycogen levels. The glycogen amounts within the muscles would be very low leaving the boxer feeling tired and weak, which would obviously affect his performance in the ring.

Many boxers when desperate to lose weight will try to reduce the fluid from their body. They will attempt this by trying to sweat the extra kilos off. Training whilst wearing a sweat suit or just plain plastic bin liners is one way boxers will often try to reduce fluid from their body, as is sitting in a sauna for an hour or so.

These types of methods will reduce weight, but it is only water that is being lost; one or two glasses of fluid and the weight will be regained. These are desperate measures and are usually the last resort to make the weight. It is totally unadvisable to try to lose weight in this way, as it will leave the boxer dehydrated. If he is in this predicament he will not be able to drink fluids until after the weigh-in, which will not allow sufficient time to re-hydrate. Sweating is a good thing, as it is the body's natural cooling system and saunas are a

great way to relax and relieve nervous tension, but it can be a dangerous practice to try and reduce too much fluid too close to the bout in an effort to make weight.

Nutrition

The basic nutrients found in the diet consists of carbohydrates, protein, fats, water, alcohol, fibre vitamins and minerals. The four basic food groups that make up the diet are:

- Fruit and vegetables
- Meat and any other proteins
- Grains
- Milk, dairy products.

To the athlete the diet is vital in the preparation for their competition, as the body needs to be fuelled with the correct consumption of healthy food. The trained sports nutritionist will usually advise a food plan designed for the athlete to consist of approximately 60 per cent carbohydrates, 30 per cent protein and 10 per cent fats. Many of the 'fad' diets would advocate reducing carbohydrate intake in the attempt to lose weight, but to the athlete carbohydrates are one of their main sources of energy. For a person who does not exercise or trains moderately two to three times a week, eating too many carbohydrates in their diet could increase the chances of unwanted weight gain. Boxers, as we have already established, usually have to maintain their weight, so eating the right type of carbohydrates is important as it plays such a large role in the fuelling of the body to withstand the type of training plan endured. To perform a high-intensive training routine, the boxer must have energy and the higher the intensity the more energy will be required. When training, the muscles will receive much of their energy from the stores of carbohydrates within the cells of the muscles and liver. This carbohydrate is known as glycogen. Once stores of muscle glycogen deplete, the boxer's ability to train will be severely affected.

The types of carbohydrates needed to produce high energy levels must come from complex

Boxers need to be strong at the weight to compete and have good punch resistance.

carbohydrates, as opposed to simple carbohydrates. Complex carbohydrates are found in starchy, wholegrain and grain products. High-fibre foods such as wholemeal bread, wholemeal pasta, cereals, pulses, vegetables and nuts, along with fruits such as apples, pears and bananas are all complex carbohydrates; they can easily be converted into glycogen. The other source of carbohydrate foods contains lots of refined or simple carbohydrates. These consist of sugars, sweet foods such as cakes, biscuits, pastries and chocolate. This type of carbohydrate has minimal nutrients and fibre and is high in fat. Complex carbohydrates play an important role in tissue building, by aiding the digestion of protein. Once carbohydrates have been eaten, they are then converted into glucose and then into nitrogen. Nitrogen is the end-product of protein and if no carbohydrate is available the liver will convert amino acids into glucose that is then turned into urea, a substance found in the urine and flushed from the body. This will cause the amino acids to have no effect in the process of tissue building.

Protein is a very important part of an athlete's diet, as it forms the building blocks of the body. If you train without sufficient amounts it will be very difficult to obtain any gains with strength and power. Protein is made up of amino acids, of which there are approximately twenty-two, with eight being considered essential. Protein foods containing all eight are known as first-class protein. Foods that are regarded as first-class protein are: eggs, milk, meat and fish. When eaten they will be broken down by the digestive system into amino acids. Amino acids aid the replacement of broken-down body tissue and cells and are vital for growth and development.

The body cannot store amino acids that are not utilized and any surplus is burnt up as energy. Four of the eight essential acids are important for tissue growth and replacement for the broken-down tissue brought on by hard training. These are: lysine, methionine, tryptophan and phenylalanine. The other four are: threonine, leucine, isoleucine and valine. The body can only absorb 20 grams of protein at any one time, so it would be more beneficial to eat four to five small meals a day. Fats are also an important nutrient, and are a good source of energy that combines important compounds and tissues that are vital for the functioning of the body. When taking part in strenuous exercise, some fats have to be included in the diet, but saturated fats should be avoided.

Many people supplement their diet by taking vitamin tablets. A good healthy diet should contain all the vitamins the body needs, but taking a certain amount of various vitamins can help towards improving performance.

Water performs numerous functions within the body and is a very important nutrient as it distributes many electrolytes within cells and throughout the body. More than 70 per cent of the body is made up of water; when water is lost through the excretion of sweat due to exercise it must be replaced. The body needs to be refuelled during a hard workout by drinking plenty of water frequently to replace the fluid lost. Not taking water on-board during training sessions can cause dehydration and heat cramps and even small amounts of water lost can seriously affect performance.

Although not absorbed by the body, fibre plays an important role in the daily diet. When food passes through the body, fibre will provide non-energy-containing bulk to the food we consume, ensuring the correct function of the gut. Sufficient fibre within the diet will help combat such conditions and illnesses as constipation, gallstones and bowel problems.

Alcohol can contribute towards providing energy as it is produced through the fermentation of carbohydrates by yeast. Unlike carbohydrates and fats it can not be utilized by the muscles to provide energy when training. It is slowly metabolized by the liver at a constant rate, so it can not produce a rapid release of energy on demand. Any energy provided through alcohol that is in excess of the body's usual energy requirement is stored as fat or used by the liver to supply energy. For the boxer or the athlete alcohol provides very little value to their diet and should be avoided.

To a competitive boxer nutrition plays a key role, not only in keeping to competition weight, but also in maintaining his energy reserves. When training at a high intensity, the boxer has to refuel

Vitamins

Vitamin A	Good for the skin and eyes. It is needed to fully utilize protein. Found in milk, egg, liver and in fish liver oils, halibut and cod liver oil.
Vitamin B	This is several vitamins within a whole complex. It is the most important vitamin for an athlete. This is obtained from foods such as desiccated liver, Brewer's yeast, wholewheat products and wheatgerm.
B Complex	As a group of vitamins, the B complex performs a variety of tasks including creating enzymes within the body to fully utilize starch, carbohydrates, fats and protein.
Vitamin C	Sometimes known as the muscle cement vitamin, due to its tightening effect upon the body tissue. It is a natural diuretic as vitamin C is not stored in the body and is lost through the excretion of excess water. A supply is needed daily and can be found mainly in fresh fruit such as, oranges, kiwi fruit and lemons. It is required for absorbing calcium and other minerals. These are mostly found in fish, liver oils and some foods, like eggs and milk.
Vitamin D	It is activated by sunlight and is formulated within the body. Minerals are not absorbed within it.
Vitamin E	Known as the vitamin of youth, as it increases virility. Also helps to increase endurance as it essentially protects oxygen, allowing the muscles to work harder without the same amount of oxygen. Found in wheatgerm, wholewheat products and some green, leafy vegetables.

Minerals

	Minerals are as important as vitamins, acting in the same way as they aid the body to utilize the food it consumes.
Calcium	The structure and the maintenance of the teeth and bones is its main function; it also helps to steady the nerves. It is very beneficial to the blood; such products as milk, cheese, butter and most dairy products will contain calcium.
Phosphorus	It works hand in hand with calcium, providing the same benefits. Meat is very high in this element.
Magnesium	Reduces cholesterol in the blood and regulates the heart rate, also strengthening muscle tissue. It is found in green vegetables, meat and dairy products.
Potassium	Beneficial to the blood supply and the nervous system, it also fills the muscles. Found in fresh fruit and some seafood.
Iron	Absorbs protein allowing it to be fully utilized. Also helps to prevent and cure anaemia by creating red blood cells. The best source of iron comes from liver and eggs.
Copper	It is closely associated with iron, aiding its absorption. Found in shellfish and nuts.
Iodine	Helps to regulate the thyroid and the body's metabolic function. It creates the correct use of starch and carbohydrates for the body. The best source can be found in fish, shellfish and kelp. This latter, in particular, contains iodine in large amounts.
Zinc	Promotes muscle growth and replaces broken-down muscle tissue caused by intensive training.

between sessions, ensuring his glycogen stores are refilled. Failing to do so will leave him short of the energy supplies he requires, which will affect his training and his ability to compete.

We have established that the boxer requires a healthy eating plan, but what should he be eating? He will need to study his diet carefully or, as expressed earlier in this chapter, seek expert advice. All boxers need various requirements from their diets, as everyone has different preferences and what works for one person may not always work

for another. Getting the balance right is the key, although a busy schedule sometimes involving two training sessions a day, often on top of a full working day, can cause difficulty in maintaining that balance. The right time to eat can also be a problem, it is just as hard training on a full stomach as it is on an empty one, when the blood sugar levels are low.

Eating small meals little and often is usually a solid guideline. Foods high in complex carbohydrates will make up a large portion of the boxer's diet, due to its energy values. Begin the day with a high carbohydrate breakfast cereal, or a bowl of porridge oats, with skimmed milk and no added sugar. A healthy high carbohydrate breakfast will help fuel the body for the day. Drinking a replacement shake mid-morning and mid-afternoon, especially after training, can be a valuable addition to the diet. These drinks are quick to make and to consume, providing all the nutrients needed from a snack. Lunch can consist of a baked potato with a variety of fillings, which could include cottage cheese, baked beans or tuna fish in brine, which is a rich source of protein. Bread should be kept to a minimum, especially when trying to reduce weight. If having a sandwich at lunchtime is more convenient, choosing the healthier wholemeal bread is the better option.

The most beneficial evening meal after training is usually protein-based, so as not to push the sugar levels up too high late in the evening. Eating large portions of carbohydrates in one meal will send the blood sugar levels soaring, causing insulin to be released from the pancreas in an attempt to push those sugar levels back down. This will leave the body feeling irritable, lethargic and within thirty minutes craving more simple carbohydrates. This can also be responsible for broken sleep. When adding carbohydrates to the evening meal keep the meals small using brown boiled rice or wholewheat pasta foods for example. Eat plenty of vegetables with your meals and try to eat more fruit. Cut down on the caffeine intake and drink plenty of water, which is still the best energy drink around. If you feel depleted of carbohydrates after training, eat a banana or a couple of Jaffa cakes, which are fast-releasing energy foods and can help increase the energy levels.

Safely Losing Weight

The intensity of the training programme followed by the boxer and a healthy eating plan should keep him at his optimum weight. It is inevitable that some will struggle to lose those last few kilos before the competition. This will obviously mean a reduction in food intake and great care and attention must be taken with his food plan. In the run-up to the bout, high carbohydrate foods like bread, pasta, potatoes and rice need to be minimized and fats completely reduced. Unfortunately with a strict diet, weight loss over the first few weeks is probably going to come from the body's carbohydrate reserves and fluids, more than fats. This will affect training, causing it to be stressful and often exhausting, which makes recovery very slow. Particular attention has to be paid towards reducing energy intake, as it can be very easy to condition the body to train and compete on low energy intake through small amounts of food. Eventually, health and performance will be affected, so it is important to attempt a gradual weight loss and always have a good intake of fluids.

Eating animal proteins, especially white meat, fish, shellfish and egg whites along with plenty of non-starchy vegetables, will help the boxer obtain the energy he requires from a low fat diet, providing him with all the healthy nutrients he will need for competition. Boxers, like most of the

Both boxers are heavyweight, with the boxer on the left, of mesomorph build and the boxer on the right, ectomorph.

population, when dieting want to lose body fat, and when building muscle through training fat will be reduced. Unfortunately muscle weighs far more than fat, so when training to make the weight the boxer has to take great care not to bulk up too much or he will not make the weight limit.

Everyone requires a certain amount of fat, like essential fat which is the percentage of lean tissue stored in the bone marrow, the heart, liver and lungs. Body Mass Index (BMI) is the height and weight ratio of an individual and by their body fat it can be seen if they are within their ideal weight guidelines. A healthy male boxer's fat percentage would normally read between 12 per cent and 16 per cent, females tend to store more body fat, so their reading would be slightly higher. There are various ways of testing body fat, such as skinfold calipers or bioelectrical impendance. Body composition is a very important component of any boxer's health and physical fitness profile.

How quickly we lose weight depends on many things like age, gender, body size and body composition. Basal metobolic rate (BMR) can also play a major part as it is the measurement of the minimal amount of energy (Kcal) that is needed to maintain physiological functions. It is directly related to the amount of lean tissue in the body. Our shapes are already designed for us at birth and we are divided up into three body types:

- Endomorph – round chubby build
- Mesomorph – muscular build
- Ectomorph – lean and thin.

Most boxers will fall between mesomorph and ectomorph, as a person with an endomorph build will unfortunately always find it difficult to lose weight.

CHAPTER 8

Planning for the Season

Many boxers need to be competing regularly to help keep them in shape and within their peak condition. As already documented earlier, a top amateur boxer can compete in over twenty bouts a year, boxing in various tournaments and championships. Some seasoned, experienced boxers may be at a stage in their careers when competing in the championships is their sole goal. This will enable them to plan their season around building towards the start of the tournament.

From competing in a club show to an international tournament, for every boxer each contest is important. He will require self-motivation to prepare himself mentally and physically in the build-up towards every bout. As each season closes, the preparation for the next season will soon begin.

The close season is the time when a busy boxer can gather his thoughts, assess his achievements over the last few months whilst weighing up the positives and the negatives. He can now plan his next season during the summer break along with his coach, setting goals and targets. First of all once the domestic season ends, he will need to rest his body and forget about boxing for a couple of weeks. A relaxing holiday where he can enjoy himself, putting on a few kilos is a great way of recharging the batteries. Once rested and feeling revitalized the boxer can start planning his programme for the approaching new season. He will need to re-evaluate himself based on the previous season, 'did he achieve all his goals?', 'did he set his targets too high or not high enough?' This he will need to discuss with the coach and together they will plan the next campaign, with his coach advising him and setting realistic targets. Once the boxer has planned in his mind what he will be attempting to achieve in the forthcoming season, he then can motivate himself and look ahead to a new training regime. This is the time to try out new training methods, experimenting, not only with new exercises but also with various nutrional plans. Light training will need to be taken to get the muscles working again, as de-training occurs within approximately two to three weeks following no exercise whatsoever. A trained body will soon regain basic fitness, but too much inactivity can cause returning to training quite a painful experience. In the early part of the close season, fitness can be maintained within a minimum of three work-outs per week. Most clubs will keep their gyms open during the summer months, allowing the more dedicated boxers to do light training to maintain their fitness level. Steady pace road work will help build up endurance and off season is a good opportunity to build strength and power with a weight-training programme. Boxing training will be light with emphasis on technique, skill and fault-finding, giving the boxer and coach time to strengthen and correct any weakness or flaws that arose during the previous competitive phase. Six weeks before the new campaign with the miles back in the legs, strength and power built up and the fault-finding session completed, training intensity will be increased. This is the preparation phase for the boxer, slowly regaining fitness while reducing any extra kilos that may have been gained over the last few months.

The domestic season begins in September and the early season phase should now see the boxers start to reach a reasonable level of fitness, as training will begin to increase in intensity and sparring will be raised a level. Many clubs at around this time will stage exhibition bouts between club members, providing an excellent opportunity for the boxers to shed the ring rust and have some light competition against team-mates. For a novice boxer looking

Running is one of the most effective ways of rebuilding base fitness.

bouts will have helped finely tune the boxer to peak at the most important part of the year. This is when the pre-season goals and targets have been set, be it winning an area title or peaking for a local home show in front of friends and family. Having reached a high level of fitness each boxer now has to structure his training around staying at that level without over-peaking.

If the boxer has looked sharp in the gym, sparred regularly and has suffered no injuries or illnesses, he will usually be ready. All coaches have their own methods of training and their own particular style of preparing each of their boxers for a bout. He will be the main person who oversees his charge's training, whilst assessing his strengths and weaknesses and it is he who will be in the corner with his boxer during the bout. Most clubs' training routines will usually follow a similar pattern and their routine during the competition phase at peak season is the most important of any boxer's training schedule. During this period when the boxer is competing regularly, training needs to be maintained between hard training and steady training, whilst not over-training. In the early part of the season hard training is not an issue, as the boxer rebuilds strength and stamina in readiness for his first few bouts. Peak season will see bouts coming thick and fast and most boxers will by then be in peak condition, making each contest usually very competitive.

towards his first contest, this is an excellent way of introducing them to performing in front of a crowd, boxing against someone whom he would have sparred with many times before in the gym. These are exhibition bouts with no winners or losers, but they are a valuable way of retuning the mind and body towards competition.

As mid-season approaches the boxer should always be constantly prepared and fully fit, ready to compete on a regular basis, with his running schedule structured towards interval and hill reps. His weight-training programme can still be one of the components of this groundwork, aiming towards keeping the level of strength required, whilst not trying to improve upon it, by increasing the poundage on the lifts. During peak season more emphasis on timed circuits and plyometric style training will be required for this phase of his training. All the workouts now should be specifically aimed at competition preparation.

Peak Season Training

By the time peak season comes around boxers should now be fully conditioned and ready to step up the competition. This is the time when the championships will be well under way and club shows will be more frequent. Early and mid-season

Close and early season is a good time to build strength and power with weight-training exercises, such as bench press.

Technique training with the coach is vital in the boxer's preparation towards his contest.

rebuilding endurance and stamina, whilst also strength training. Road work will be stepped up from the steady-state running of the off season to faster pace short-distance runs between 4 and 5km.

Mid Season

Runs will start to include intervals and hill reps, with maybe one day for a recovery run. At this point in the season, training may need to be stepped up to running in the morning and strength training in the afternoon, depending on the individual time restrictions. Boxing sessions will usually continue in the same structured way each week, concentrating on explosive power and fitness, whilst incorporating skill and technique work into the programme.

The coach obviously prefers to know well in advance when his boxer will be competing, so this will enable him to gauge his training around the contest allowing time to get his boxer within the preferred weight, whilst tapering off the training as the contest approaches. Unfortunately there will be occasions when a boxer will only receive a couple of or even one day's notice before a bout. No coach would ask a boxer to compete on such short notice if he did not believe he was fit enough and ready, but the final decision must always be left to the boxer himself. He may feel that he is not physically prepared, but more often than not this can be a mental attitude and have little to do with his fitness. The boxer will always feel there is something extra he should have done to prepare for a bout, such as extra running or more sparring, but competing with less time to prepare mentally can often be an advantage. To have little time to build up nerves and self-doubt can work in the boxer's favour.

Early Season

Training will not alter that much throughout the term, there will of course be more emphasis on

Varied work on the bags is an important part of any boxer's training. Having the boxer alternate between long, medium and short range will help him prepare for any opponent.

Sparring in most clubs will have stepped up a level, although technique and condition sparring should still be part a of any boxer's routine.

Peak Season

Training will now see the boxer constantly ticking over as he is by this time hopefully fit and as good as he is going to be for this term. It will be the trainer's job to help keep him at this level. Weight-training for power may now need to be sacrificed for extra timed or target circuits or plyometric sessions. The following devised sample weekly training programme is for a senior boxer in peak condition during the most competitive phase of the season. Specific boxing training needs to be performed a minimum of three days a week. Sparring can be replaced during one of the sessions with technique work on the pads with the coach.

Training days in the gym will depend on the opening hours of the club. Remember this training schedule is a guideline and will not suit all boxers, or be favoured by all coaches, who must have the final say on the boxer's training regime. It is just as important not to overtrain and if your body is telling you it is tired and jaded, take a day or two off from training. Always listen to your body.

Specific Boxing Training	
Day One	10min warm-up
	4 × 2min rounds – Skipping
	4 × 2min rounds – Sparring (open
	and technique)
	2 × 2min rounds – Pad Work
	4 × 2min rounds – Various kinds of
	Bag Work
	4 × 2min rounds – Shadow Boxing

Choose from ton up, timed or target circuits, plyometric sessions.

	5–10min cool down
Day Two	Running – Interval Sprints
Day Three	Boxing Training
Day Four	Running – Hill Reps
Day Five	Boxing Training
Day Six	REST
Day Seven	Recovery Run 4–5km or Technique Session with the Coach

Building towards the Bout

To prepare yourself physically and mentally in the build-up towards a bout is vitally important, and boxers will have their own methods of getting themselves up and ready to compete. Going into the ring under-prepared could be the difference between a win or a loss in the boxer's record book. In an ideal world the boxer will have plenty of notice as to when he is boxing and even some knowledge about his opponent. As already stated, boxers can compete with very little notice and know little about their opponent, but they need to be in a constant state of readiness.

As with most aspects of boxing, the build-up towards the bout starts at the gym where once the boxer knows when and hopefully who he will be competing against, he can begin his preparation. The coach will do his job by guiding his charge through his training, whilst monitoring his weight, but in a busy gym the boxer himself must take responsibility for his own behaviour outside the gym. Although the coach plays a huge role in the development of his club members, it is not possible for him go home with each and everyone of them once the gym closes.

If the boxer has approximately four weeks' notice before his next contest, this will allow him time to focus on his bout and tailor the training towards the contest. The intensity of his training will be performed at the same level until approximately five days before he boxes. Having knowledge of his opponent will help him devise a strategy to combat against his style. This he can try and achieve by working closely with his coach, trying to spar with someone of a similar style. If he is an orthodox boxer and his opposition is a southpaw, he will then need to try and spar with as many southpaws as possible, or if he is up against a stockier, strong counter-puncher, sparring with someone of the same build and style will be a major advantage.

Once the boxer has a date confirmed for his next bout, his whole focus will be concentrated towards that contest. His training now has a purpose and his attitude towards all the hard work he has put in will change. The weeks or days before his contest will be all about the opponent and during every round of bags, shadow boxing and sparring he will have a mental picture of how he is going to win. Almost every aspect of a boxer's training routine in the gym will be against the clock. The two-minute rounds become an important part of the amateur boxer's life, with many of them possessing their own mental clock inside their heads. Boxers need to set their own pace during each round and the final thirty seconds of a round could prove to be vital. If he feels he is behind on points, the boxer will try to increase his work rate for those last thirty seconds, especially if it is the final round.

By attempting to sustain the pressure on his opponent for the final quarter of each round this will help to finish the rounds strongly and hopefully on top. This can demoralize an opponent, giving the attacking boxer a slight psychological advantage. This is where the fitness of a boxer will be really tested, as all-out efforts such as these can be exhausting on the body and he will only have one minute in between rounds to recover. The boxer must have confidence in his stamina and recovery rate to attempt such tactics and he will need to have practised them many times in the gym. During training the coaches will be constantly calling out 'thirty seconds, twenty seconds and last ten', which will help the boxer pace his round.

In a bout the corner men are not permitted to call out instructions during the contest, so if a game plan or tactics have been devised then some coaches may be placed amongst the crowd. This will give them the opportunity to call out certain instructions to their charges during the bout, leaving the corner man to do his job in between rounds. This is when a good relationship and regular communication between the boxer and his coaches are essential. Some boxers will be oblivious to what is taking place outside the ring, but just a call of 'last thirty seconds' or 'last twenty' could be enough to put them into overdrive and finish the round on top.

As the last few days before his contest approaches, the boxer begins to taper his training. Training will now become less physical, with emphasis on speed and movement as he must keep his work rate flowing whilst decreasing heavy training. He will have usually been ready way before the day of the bout and he must now keep himself in peak contest condition. Experienced boxers will always know when they are ready and when to taper off their training and by how much, but for the first-bout novice it is not so easy. This will be a whole new experience to him and he must rely heavily on his coach's guidance. It should be drilled into every up-and-coming novice the importance of preparation for their first few contests. A boxer competing in his first contest will need to have rehearsed competition day many times before it actually becomes a reality. That is – what training they should have done in the final few days; how much sleep they should have on the night before; and what they need to eat on the day. All these questions will have to be answered to help the boxer mentally prepare, so he can see what works for him.

A week before the bout is not the time to experiment with any new training methods or nutrition, as the boxer needs to know well in advance what his best preparation is and to keep to it. This is not to say that improvements cannot be made, but they should be tried and tested during pre-season. If training has gone to plan, the boxer's weight should be well within his weight category limit. By weighing about 2kg (4lb) under the minimum weight limit, this allows the boxer to re-fuel the body adequately. As he tapers his training he is reducing the rate at which he uses glycogen and by eating more high energy foods, the body will be replenished. As he gradually tapers off from training in the final week before the contest and eats more complex carbohydrates, this will ensure that his glycogen stores are increased. Although it is imperative to re-fuel the body whilst keeping rehydrated, care has to be taken not to go over the weight limit or to gorge at mealtimes, keeping to smaller, more frequent meals.

The day before the contest some boxers will rest totally, while others may feel the need to do light exercise like a steady run or a light shadow boxing session in the ring, mentally going over the bout and practising their strategy. What the boxer will

Shadow boxing in the ring, going over the up-and-coming bout, will help the boxer mentally prepare for his contest.

not want to do is to have a hard training session and restrict his food intake because he is over his weight limit. When the day of the bout finally arrives he should be fully fit and well within his weight limit. If he is in full-time employment he might take a day's holiday especially if it is a championship match, while others may prefer to work to help take their mind off the up-and-coming bout. Rest is a very important component of every boxer's preparation and all through his training he should have made sure he has received adequate sleep. Hard training will usually ensure that the athlete has little trouble sleeping, but it can also have the opposite effect, causing him to be agitated and restless, especially the night before a bout.

A healthy mind is as important as a healthy body, as boxing is as much a thinking sport as it is a physical one. Training may have gone perfectly to plan, with the boxer looking sharp during each session, whilst coming in well within his weight limit with no physical problems. Although he may look in great condition, come the day of the bout if his mental attitude is not right, he may have lost before he has even reached the venue. Many factors can

contribute to his mind not being fully focused, such as problems at home, school, work or even letting nerves take over. All boxers get nervous before entering the ring and experiencing some nerves can be a positive sign. Being slightly edgy before a bout will help a boxer maintain their focus, but it is important not to let those nerves be overwhelming. If a boxer becomes too scared, he should not be in the ring, as fear will take over his logical thinking. Every athlete will at some stage during their career have been scared but it has to be controlled.

Other issues such as depression and self-doubt could lead to the boxer losing concentration. A good coach should be able to recognize whether or not the boxer's mind is totally focused on the sport. If there are any concerns, the coach and the boxer should talk openly in an effort to resolve any underlying problems. A boxer needs to retain positive thinking, whilst possessing the three qualities of self-esteem, self-confidence, and self-motivation. Having a positive attitude will help any boxer through the competitive phase of the season. When self-doubt and negative thoughts start to filter into the boxer's mind, he has usually allowed himself to be beaten. Once self-esteem has been gained, the boxer will have pride in what he has achieved and this will, in turn, give the boxer confidence.

Self-confidence is essential, although being over-confident and underestimating an opponent can be dangerous. No one should enter into any sport if they have no motivation to compete. It is motivation that drives all athletes in their quest to perform well and to the best of their ability. Coaches will play their role in motivating boxers, but the individual must be self-motivated before entering into any competitive contest. On the day of the contest the boxer will experience a whole host of emotions, mentally going through the process of beating the opposition one moment and the next having concerns about any previous conditions or injuries that may affect the outcome of the contest. This is all part of the nervous process and this is when a positive attitude needs to take over.

When arriving at the venue, the coach and the boxer will need to find the dressing room, where the boxer will undress and be weighed. Presuming

Once the bell sounds, the boxers are on their own.

The author is all smiles as he celebrates a win in the dressing room. Coach Dennis Jackson looks to prepare his next boxer.

the boxer's weight is within the category limit, the doctor will then look at the boxer's medical card and carry out a quick medical check. If the boxer appears fit to box he will then wait. This is one of the worst aspects of the sport for the boxers, as the waiting can be up to three to four hours before entering the ring. The boxer will have his own ways of passing the time before being called upon – some will sit in a corner listening to their iPods, others will find a quiet space and try to sleep and some will keep on the move watching the other

Hearing the master of ceremonies (MC) announce your name and having the referee raise your arm makes all the hard work worth it.

bouts and engaging in conversation with their team-mates. This is all part of each individual boxer's preparation. Eventually 'kitted out' and 'gloved up', the call will be received. After a quick warm-up usually on the pads, the boxer and the corner men will take the long walk to the ring.

Basic Rules

As with every sports person a boxer needs to familiarize himself with the rules of his sport. The coach will have educated him on the basic rules with emphasis on one in particular, obey the referee at all times. During a bout the referee will have three words of command, upon any of which boxer shall step back before continuing.

1. 'Stop' when ordering the boxers to stop boxing.
2. 'Box' when ordering the boxers to continue boxing.
3. 'Break' when breaking a clinch.

Like most sports, amateur boxing has many rules and regulations and, also like most sports, they can change quite regularly. The important fundamentals of the sport remain the same and a boxer must learn the rules that will affect him mostly in competition – for example, rules such as once a boxer has scored a knock-down or a standing count against his opponent, he must retreat to a neutral corner. This is a rule all boxers will know, but the novice boxer who is caught up in the excitement of seeing his opponent on the floor, can sometimes forget. Those few seconds of indecision could give his opponent valuable seconds to recover, as the referee will not be able to take up the count until the boxer is in the neutral corner. There are rules that may not be so obvious, but they must also be obeyed, such as the use of grease or Vaseline not being allowed to be worn on the face to help prevent cuts or that all boxers should be cleanshaven, although it is permissible to have a moustache. A boxer must have an understanding of what are deemed as fouls in a contest. Only three warnings may be given to each boxer during a contest. A third warning brings automatic disqualification.

The following are fouls:

- Hitting below the belt, holding, butting and kicking with foot or knee.
- Hits or blows with head, shoulders, forearm, elbow, throttling the opponent, pressing with arm or elbow in opponent's face, pressing the head of the opponent back over the ropes.
- Hitting with open glove, the inside of the glove, the wrist or the hand.
- Hits landing on the back of the opponent, especially any blows to the back of the neck, head or kidneys.
- Pivot blows.
- Attack whilst holding the ropes or making any unfair use of the ropes.
- Lying on, wrestling and throwing in a clinch.
- An attack on an opponent who is down or is in the act of rising.
- Holding.
- Holding and hitting or pulling and hitting.
- Holding or locking the opponent's arm or head or pushing an arm underneath the arm of an opponent.
- Ducking below the belt of the opponent in a manner dangerous to the opponent.
- Completely passive defence by means of double cover and intentionally fouling to avoid a blow.

- Useless, aggressive or offensive utterances during the round.
- Not stepping back when ordered to 'Break'.
- Attempting to strike the opponent immediately after the referee has ordered 'Break' and before taking a step back.
- Assaulting or behaving in an aggressive manner towards a referee at any time.
- Spitting out a gumshield or for any other act the referee may deem improper.

The Risk of Injuries

It would be quite naïve for anyone to think that any sport where points are gained by punching your opponent was completely safe. As with any sport that involves physical activity, the standard strains and pulls can occur, but contact sports like boxing will obviously have a higher risk of more serious injuries. Most injuries will be around the face and head, but they are usually superficial, such as minor cuts or bruises. Due to the wearing of headguards, severe cuts are very rare in amateur boxing.

Other areas where injuries can occur are around the midriff and body, especially within the rib area. If the boxer is knocked out or the referee has stopped the contest due to a boxer sustaining a hard blow to the head causing him to be unable to continue, he will not be permitted to box for twenty-eight days and a second knock-out will be eighty-four days, with a third knock-out twelve months, if all three knock-outs have been within one year. Serious damage such as concussion or even brain damage can occur, but it is very rare.

Boxers with short-sightedness can sometimes be prone to a detached retina, due to the thin retina being pulled off the back of the eyeball by pressure waves set when the eye is hit. So anyone who is short-sighted or has a family history of retina detachment should seek the advice of their GP or an eye specialist before boxing.

The safety precautions in amateur boxing are very stringent and most injuries can be solved with an ice pack and rest. As long as the guidelines are followed it is as safe as any other physical sport.

CHAPTER 9

The Future of Amateur Boxing in England

By the end of the 1970s amateur boxing in England was very popular with approximately 900 registered ABA clubs in the country. The National Championship always had great coverage by the media and boxing shows were shown frequently around the nation. During the 1990s many clubs went into decline as the small amateur clubs found difficulty in raising the funds to keep them afloat.

The domestic showpiece of the year, the ABA finals, used to be held at a packed Royal Albert Hall or the Wembley Arena, with every bout shown on mainstream television on the same night. As sponsorship for these events started to dry up the venues and attendance became smaller and amateur boxing began to lose its appeal. The amateur code has always lived slightly in the shadows of the professional side of the sport, but fans of the professional game always had a good knowledge and appreciation of the amateur sport. By the time the millennium had arrived the ABAE had decreased to 620 registered clubs. For any sport to attract more people and entice sponsorship, it must gain international success.

The Amateur International Boxing Association (AIBA), was first founded in 1946 and was made up from twenty-three associations, mainly from Europe. It has now grown into a worldwide association with multi-nation tournaments measuring the success of every amateur boxing nation. To the general public, success at the Olympics is what really brings a sport to the forefront of their attention. Winning a medal at the games brings not only success and recognition to the athlete, but also to the sport they represent. A sport is gauged by the success of its participants, and as highlighted in earlier chapters, Britain as a nation has had little success in winning boxing medals. When Audley Harrison gave England their first gold medal since 1968, in the Sydney Olympics 2000, it should have provided the springboard that the amateur association needed to build a strong team for Athens 2004.

One year later in the World Championships in Belfast 2001, David Haye won a silver medal and Carl Froch a bronze, giving England their first medals ever in a senior World Championship. A year later at the Commonwealth Games in Manchester 2002 England won two gold, three silver and two bronze medals. After ten medals in three multi-nation tournaments over two years, it would have been anticipated that the future of English amateur boxing would have been very bright indeed. Unfortunately two years later when the Athens Olympics 2004 came around, England had one single entrant, 17-year-old Amir Khan. By the time 2004 had arrived the amateurs had lost medal hopes Haye and Froch to the professional game and for English boxers to qualify for the Olympics as previously documented it is very difficult. England had to qualify through the European stages that can consist of sixteen former Soviet Union boxers.

Amateur boxing in Russia, like Cuba, is state-funded and this along with their disciplined training regime and winning mentality produces medal winners. Amir Khan went to Athens as England's

A star of today with two stars of tomorrow. 2006 Commonwealth Games gold medallist Frankie Gavin poses with two-up-and-coming schoolboy boxers, Conor Tierney and Jack Davies.

amateur code, but the professional sport will also reach wider audiences.

Boxers who win Olympic medals become household names, so they are already popular before they turn professional. The media interest that surrounded Khan when he returned from Athens proves this.

Amateur boxing is starting to build up its profile again in this country, as BBC sport gives regular coverage of domestic and multi-nation championships. Boxing development officers are one of the forward-thinking additions that the ABAE have put into place. Paul King, who is the Chief Executive of the ABAE, was development officer for Liverpool and through his efforts he has helped revitalize boxing in the city. Boxing in Liverpool is thriving, producing many national champions and a bronze medal in the 2005 World Championships in China due to Neil Perkins' efforts.

Cities all over England are starting to follow the example set by Liverpool, by having boxing development officers of their own. This is a full-time job that requires a close working relationship with clubs and coaches of the area, increasing participation, performance and funding.

In the 2006 Commonwealth Games in Brisbane, England had six boxers reaching the finals, winning five gold medals, one silver medal and two bronze medals. This made England the top boxing nation in Brisbane and a lot of credit must go to the national coach Terry Edwards.

Top amateur boxers in Britain and Ireland are now at last beginning to receive funding, allowing them to concentrate on their sport. Amateur boxing in the four nations is evolving and looking stronger and hopefully by the 2012 Olympics in London, we will produce one of the top boxing nations.

sole boxing representative and returned with a silver medal. Of all the athletes who represented Britain in the sporting events in the Olympics, Khan was the only true amateur with no sponsorship or income coming from his sport. Due to his success the ABAE offered him an annual income in an attempt to keep him as an amateur boxer for the next Olympics. Khan decided to turn professional, but due to his success, interest in the sport has grown. England possesses the talent and high standard of coaching to match any nation and if it had the funding of sports, such as swimming or rowing, our boxers would be up amongst the medal winners. Unfortunately for the amateur sport, most of its top boxers turn professional at the first opportunity. However, by keeping the boxers in the amateurs long enough to produce world-beating squads, this will not only help the

Appendix: The Rules of Boxing

Many of the rules of amateur boxing have been covered earlier in this book. Below are some important rules and conditions set by the ABAE; for a full list of the ABA rules, visit www.abae.co.uk.

ABAE coaches and officials will not be allowed to register with the Amateur Boxing Association of England until their name appears on the ABAE Criminal Records Bureau disclosure list.

Volunteers who wish to be active in an amateur boxing club are also subject to the same conditions. Coaches and officials MUST carry their ABAE registration cards when they attend tournaments as proof of the conditions stated. The card must be produced if requested by the OIC (official-in-charge).

1. An official-in-charge. Referees, Judges, Timekeeper, Clerk of Scales, MCs and Medical Officers shall be appointed by the Associations or Divisions for all tournaments. Such officials must be:

   a) CRB cleared and registered with the ABAE for the current season
   b) Qualified by examination (by a member of the ABAE Referees & Judges Commission)
   c) Be on the appropriate Association list of OICs, Referees & Judges and timekeepers

Any official who has been inactive for three or more years shall be re-assessed by written, oral and practical examination before being allowed to resume his duties.

2. It is the responsibility of those staging the tournament to provide a Medical Officer, a competent Master of Ceremonies (who must be ABAE qualified), a Recorder and all necessary Stewards.
3. Only in exceptional circumstances will the OIC allow officials who are also qualified coaches to act in both roles at the same tournament.

Weigh-in

1. At all tournaments a weigh-in will take place and must be overseen by the official-in-charge or an official from the Referees & Judges list who has been appointed as Clerk of Scales. Boxers must produce their ME3 at the weigh-in.
2. No boxer will be allowed to take part in a contest where the weight differential is greater than that allowed in his championship weight category.
3. Boxers under the age of 17 must wear shorts or underpants when weighing in.
4. Female boxers must wear shorts and a singlet top when they weigh in.
5. Only one boxer and one coach are allowed to attend the scales.

Medical

1. A qualified Medical Officer must examine intending competitors. No competitor will be permitted to box unless certified as being medically fit to do so.
2. Any boxer that has been debarred from boxing on medical grounds shall not compete until passed fit to do so by a medical officer nominated by their association/division.

3. No boxer shall be allowed to take part in a contest if they wear any dressing on a cut, wound, laceration or blood swelling on their scalp or face, including the nose and ears.

4. A boxer will not be allowed to compete unless they produce their ME3. The ME3 clearly states the classification of the boxer and displays on the inside cover the expiry date of his/her medical examination period.

5. Female boxers must sign the official ABAE medical disclaimer in the presence of the examining doctor.

6. From the date of their thirtieth birthday boxers must have a full medical examination and complete a new ME1 every year until they reach the age of thirty-four, after which they are not allowed to box.

7. Boxers who have not competed for a period of twelve months cannot box until they have completed an ME1 and undergone the full medical process.

8. A boxer's five-year medical (one year in the case of a thirty-year-old) must not take place at a tournament.

9. If the doctor believes that a bout should be stopped, he/she shall advise the jury chairman and/or OIC and, if agreed, the bout shall be stopped to allow the doctor to examine the boxer. The referee will then be advised on whether the bout can continue.

Illegal Substances/Drug Abuse

10. All drug testing is carried out by the Drug Control Unit of UK Sport and according to IOC protocols for the Olympic Games. This means that testing can occur at random at training as well as at competition. The list of prohibited substances is updated frequently and the latest lists can be obtained from the UK Sport website. As changes in testing methods occur these are announced on the UK Sport website. Refusal to take a test is considered a positive test and penalties are applied according to UK Sport regulations.

11. Medical Controls.

As laid down in the Medical Aspects of Boxing

12. Attendance of Doctor.

A qualified doctor of medicine, so approved, MUST be in attendance throughout all tournaments. Should the doctor be called away from the ringside at any time, the tournament must be suspended whilst he/she is absent.

The doctor has to confirm, at the time of appointment, that he/she is equipped for, and is competent and confident in, airway resuscitation, and is prepared to officiate without paramedical assistance. Otherwise a person or team so equipped and qualified must also be in attendance.

The nearest NHS Accident & Emergency Unit, together with the responsible ambulance station, must be informed of the full address, date and time of the tournament.

Junior Boxers

1. A boxer is a junior, and is eligible to hold a ME3, from their eleventh birthday until the date of their seventeenth birthday.

   a) Boxers under the age of seventeen years cannot concede more than twelve months in age

   b) It is recommended that junior boxers do not concede age, weight and experience in a contest. The final decision for any contest is the responsibility of the official in charge

3. Unless the conditions for championships or other authorized events prescribe otherwise, the duration of bouts for junior boxers will be as follows:

Both boxers aged over eleven years and under fourteen years – 3 × 1.5-minute rounds.
One boxer aged thirteen years and the other fourteen years – 3 × 1.5-minute rounds.

Both boxers ages fourteen years –
3 × 2-minute rounds.
One boxer fourteen years and the other
fifteen years – 3 × 2-minute rounds
Both boxers fifteen or over – 3
or 4 × 2-minute rounds (male boxers only)
All contests will have an interval of 1 minute
between rounds.

4. a) Boxers under the age of sixteen
        years shall not be allowed to box at
        tournaments after 10:30pm
    b) It is recommended that boxers aged 16
        should not box after 11pm
    c) Boxers up to the season of their
        seventeenth birthday are allowed to box a
        maximum fourteen contests per
        season, excluding championship and
        internationals

Senior Boxers

1. Boxers are seniors from the date of their
   seventeenth birthday to the date of their
   thirty-fourth birthday after which they can no
   longer box. A seventeen-year-old can box a
   sixteen-year-old provided that there is no more
   than twelve months' difference in their age.

A thirty-four-year-old boxer must return his/her
ME3 to the association/divisional registrar for
cancellation. The cancelled ME3 can be sent
back to the boxer if they wish to keep it as a
souvenir.

2. There shall be three classes of senior boxers.
   The appropriate classification must be stamped
   on the boxers ME3.

Novice

A novice is a boxer who has not competed in an
open senior championship. A novice boxer must
not compete against an open class boxer other
than in recognized championships.

Intermediate

An intermediate is a boxer who has won a Novice
Class 'B' (Class 'C' in the case of females) title or
competed in an open senior championship but has
not won an association title.

Open

An open boxer is one who has:

    a) Competed in and won a senior
        championship at association level or above.
    b) Boxed at senior level for his country.

An Association Executive Committee may up-
grade a boxer who, in its opinion, is clearly above
the prevailing standard for their current level of
classification.
  Similarly, a boxer may be down-graded if their
ability, in its opinion, is below the standard prevailing in their current classification.

3. Senior boxers will box 3 × 2-minute rounds
   and may box 4 × 2-minute rounds. In open
   championships and internationals they will
   box 4 × 2-minute rounds. In every case there
   will be an interval of one minute between
   rounds.
4. A senior boxer may participate in a maximum
   of eighteen contests per season excluding
   championships and internationals.
5. Boxers who have relinquished their
   professional license and have not had more
   than four professional bouts may rejoin
   amateur boxing as boxers, but cannot
   compete in the ABAE championships in the
   first season following their return. Written
   proof must be supplied by the BBBC.

Championships

1. The ABAE Championships are open to
   British and non-British nationals.
   Non-British nationals must have held an

ABAE ME3 for a period of 1 year prior to the championships.

2. Boxers entering any ABAE championship must be members of a club or organization affiliated to the ABAE. They must represent the club etc. of which they were a member preceding the championships in which they engaged.

3. A boxer age seventeen or eighteen can choose to box in either the junior or senior championships, but not both. Their ME3 must be clearly marked with the championship they have competed in.

4. Entry must be made on the form provided by the ABAE. The form must be signed by the entrant (and, if under eighteen endorsed by their parent or guardian) who will be held responsible for the accuracy of the statements made on the form. A closing date for receipt of entry forms should be set prior to the first stage of the championships.

5. To be awarded a national title a boxer must compete in at least one stage (this includes the final) of the championship.

6. In all championships boxers in the RED corner cannot wear a BLUE vest or BLUE headguard and boxers in the BLUE corner cannot wear a RED vest or RED headguard.

7. The ABAE championships will be contested as follows:

   a) Regional Divisional Championships
   b) Regional Association Championships
   c) Zone Championships
   d) Nation quarter finals – The winners of an Association Championship will compete in one of the quarter finals decided annually by the Technical & Rules Commission
   e) National Semi Finals in which the winners of the quarter finals will compete
   f) National Finals in which the winners of the semi finals will compete
   g) Four Nations Cup (Great Britain & Irish Championships) in which the winners of the finals will compete for their club against boxers from Ireland, Scotland and Wales.

Bibliography and Further Reading

Books

The Amateur Boxing Association of England Official Handbook (Media Ltd).

Andre, Sam and Fleischer, Nat, *A Pictorial History of Boxing* (Hamlyn Publishing Group Ltd, 1982).

Angstn, Peg and Ferrari, Mary Beth (eds), *Aerobics* (Aerobics and Fitness Association of America, 1988).

Hickey, Kevin, *Boxing – The Amateur Boxing Association, Coaching Manual* (Kaye and Ward Ltd, 1980).

Hugman, Barry J. (ed), *The British Boxing Board of Control, Boxing Year Book* (Queen Anne Press).

Williams, J. P. R (consultant editor), *Sports Injuries Handbook* (Willow Books, 1987).

Wooton, Dr Steve, *Nutrition and Sports Performance* (The National Coaching Foundation, 1985).

Magazines

Boxing Monthly
Boxing News

Websites

ABA Club Finder – www.boxingnewonline.net

The Amateur Boxing Association of England Limited – www.abae.co.uk

Gary Blower – www.thestudiofitnesscompany. co.uk

Useful Addresses

International Amateur Boxing Association
135 Westervelt Place
Creskill
NJ 07626
USA

Tel: 001-201-567-3117

United Kingdom

Amateur Boxing Association of England Ltd (ABAE)
Colin Brown
Hon. Secretary
National Sport Centre
Crystal Place
London
SE19 2BB

Tel: 020-8778-0251
Fax: 020-8778-9324
Email: hq@abac.org.uk

Tel: 00353-1-4533371
Fax: 00353-1-4540777
Email: iaba@eircom.net

Welsh ABA
Jack Watkins
Hon. Secretary
8 Erw Wen
Rhiwbina
Cardiff
CF4 6JW

Tel: 02920-623-566

Amateur Boxing Scotland
Donald Campbell
Administrator
Strathdonan
High Street
Elgin
IV30 1AH

Tel: 01343-544718
Email: donald@absboxmg.fsnet.co.uk

Schools ABA
Dudley Savill
11 Beaconsfield Road
Ealing
London
W5 5JE

Tel: 020-8840-5519

Referees and Judges (England)
John Ball
6 Saddlers Way
Raunds
Northants
NN9 6RS

Tel: 01933-625821

Boxing Board of Control Ltd
(Professional Boxing)
Simon Block
General Secretary
The Old Library
Trinity Street
Cardiff
CF10 1BH

Tel: 02920-367000
Fax: 02920-367019
Email: sblock@bbbofc.com
Website: www.bbbofc.com

Ireland

Irish ABA
Sean Crowley
Hon. Secretary
National Boxing Stadium
South Circular Road
Dublin 2
Ireland

USA

United States Amateur Boxing, Inc.
(USA Boxing)
1 Olympic Piazz
Colarado Springs
CO 80909
USA

Tel: 001-719-578-4506
Fax: 001-719-632-3426
Email: usaboxing@aol.com

Canada

Canadian Amateur Boxing Association
888 Belfast Road
Ottawa
Ontario
K1G 0Z6
Canada

Tel: 001-613-238-7700
Fax: 001-613-238-1600
Email: acaba@boxing.ca

Glossary

Active rest   Light mobility exercise used by athletes on rest days.

Blocking   Used to stop advancing punches with the palm of the glove.

Cardiovascular training   Exercises designed to improve and strengthen the heart and lungs.

Combination Punching   A cluster of two or more punches .

Counter Punching   A punch or punches thrown immediately after successfully defending against an attack.

Covering   How a defending boxer guards himself against an attack, using full cover, half cover or cross-over cover.

Drawing   Used to entice opponents to attack, leaving openings in their guard.

Ducking   Dropping the body below an on-coming punch, by bending the knees.

Ectomorph   Body type of a person with a lean and thin build.

Endomorph   Body type of a person who has a round, chubby build.

Fartlek   A Swedish term for speed play during running.

Feinting   A move used to confuse and disorientate opponents whilst creating openings for attack.

Forearm blocks   Used as a defence against hooks and uppercuts to the body.

Gliding   Footwork manoeuvre bringing a boxer outside his opponents guard.

Glove block   Used to defend against an uppercut to the head.

Head movement   Slipping and rolling of the head used to avoid attacking punches.

Hooks   A bent arm punch that comes around and outside the opponent's guard and view.

In-fighting   Boxing at close range, working inside the opponent's defence.

Inside wedge   Defence against body shot by dropping the arm in a sweeping motion to block the on-coming punch.

Jab   A straight-arm punch with the leading hand, mainly used for point scoring and opening the opponent's defence.

Lay back   Transferring body weight towards the rear foot, bringing the boxer out of range from an attacking punch.

Messomorph   Body type of a person with a muscular build.

Orthodox   The boxer's stance, leading with his left hand.

Parrying   A defence move against straight punches using the inside of the glove against the wrist or forearm of the attacking punch.

Punch bag PVC or leather bag used by boxers to practise punching combinations and to increase power.

Shadow boxing Boxing against an imaginary opponent to help improve techniques. Can also be performed in front of a mirror to assist with fault-finding.

Shoulder block Defence against straight right to the head, using shoulder and forearm.

Skipping Jumping rope to aid footwork and co-ordination.

Slipping Moving head inside or outside of on-coming punch.

Straight right A straight punch thrown by the orthodox boxer, as a power punch or point scorer.

Stretching Performed post-exercise to help improve flexibility, loosen tight muscles and help injury prevention.

Uppercut Punch thrown in an upright motion keeping at a 90-degree angle.

Wedge block Defence against straight punches and hooks by moving arm inside the opponent's advancing blow, forming a wedge between the elbow.

Index